PICKED UP, PATCHED UP, AND SENT HOME

Like so many people, Carl Walker has used the NHS for a number of reasons throughout his life — some serious, others less so. From being caught red-handed testing a stethoscope on himself, and (unsuccessfully) attempting to remove a friend's ingrown toenail with a pair of pliers, to the health visitor who offers guidance that soothes Carl's newborn and restores sanity to his household, the specialists who help him manage his epilepsy, and the GP who assures him the worrying lump is not cancer, here are stories that speak to the experiences of normal folk, and remind us just what an amazing thing a public national health service really is.

CARL WALKER

PICKED UP, PATCHED UP AND SENT HOME

Why I Love the NHS

Complete and Unabridged

ULVERSCROFT
Leicester

First published in Great Britain in 2015 by
Robert Hale Limited
London

First Large Print Edition
published 2016
by arrangement with
Robert Hale Limited
London

A catalogue record for this book is available
from the British Library.

ISBN 978–1–4448–2763–7

Published by
F. A. Thorpe (Publishing)
Anstey, Leicestershire

Set by Words & Graphics Ltd.
Anstey, Leicestershire
Printed and bound in Great Britain by
T. J. International Ltd., Padstow, Cornwall

This book is printed on acid-free paper

For Anna and Andrew — my specials

'The NHS will last as long as there are folk left with the faith to fight for it'
Aneurin Bevan, 1948

When I was about seven years of age I had something of an epiphany and it took my older brother rather brutally falling off his bike to provide it. Well, he didn't really brutally fall off his bike; it was more that he landed brutally. It was a swelteringly hot day on our Kilmarnock council estate and the children were racing their bikes round the block. My brother had a racer and was going at an admirable speed. He had pulled ahead of Darren Malloy and was beginning to put the hurt into a visibly tiring Derek McGill when it all went horribly wrong. He lost his back wheel on a patch of gravel strewn over one corner of the road. We went to check whether my brother was still intact and were actually surprised to find that he literally wasn't. He appeared to have lost a lump of flesh out of his right thigh. The hole was around half an inch deep and an inch and a half across. Now, in my limited experience,

1

lumps of flesh tend not to go too far as they don't have viable means of transport so, as my brother was carted off to hospital, my friends and I decided to make ourselves useful by finding the lump of flesh. It seemed like pretty much the only useful contribution we could make to this particular medical emergency.

As best as I can remember, our plan was to find the lump and take it to the hospital so that the doctors could put it back in. After all, it had no place holidaying on the concrete when it should have been in my brother's leg. What took all of us by surprise was that, despite turning that corner of the block upside down, we couldn't find the lump. We must have searched for over an hour but still no luck. We even lifted up a drain cover and looked to see whether it had scuttled off down there. After a while we gave up, sat on the kerb and tried to figure out how the lump had disappeared. Somebody suggested that maybe someone had stolen it but even at age seven we realized that, unless we had a budding Hannibal Lecter on our estate, this was quite unlikely. Maybe someone had picked it up on the sole of their shoe? Or perhaps a hungry dog had wandered by unobserved and found himself a cheeky little hors d'ouevre? As we prepared a coordinated shakedown of all the local dogs we were put out of our misery. A local adult, Mr McGruder, told us that there was no lump.

No lump? But how could that be? It was a deep hole, we saw it with our own eyes. What was this witchcraft of which he spoke? The Samaritan informed us that it was in fact a tear. The flesh had torn open in such a way that it looked like a lump was missing but the doctors would simply clean it out and stitch it back together. Now Mr McGruder liked a drink for sure and he was partial to lunchtime treats at the Charleston pub. However, on this occasion he was walking as straight as a ruler.

That doctors were able to stitch flesh was a shock. I remember sitting on the kerb in amazement at the power of these shamans who could make flesh holes disappear just by treating them like a pair of trousers that had burst over the arse (which happened to me a lot). This was a revelation indeed. Not a revelation sufficiently powerful to drive me into a nascent career in medicine but pretty profound nonetheless for a seven-year-old mind.

Thirty years on, and I still have yet to truly relinquish the sense of wonder and awe I feel in the face of the various forms of magic that can be enacted to piece us together when we start to fall apart. However, in the intervening years, my musings have acquired a degree of sophistication. When I think back, what that seven-year-old boy sitting on the kerb didn't understand was how amazing it was that even a boy from a single-parent family living on a council estate in the midst of Thatcher's Britain could receive immediate expert care that was free at the point of delivery. My brother was taken straight to hospital and was back home within two hours, stitched up, bandaged up and laughing at us for trying to find his lump. And it had not cost my family a single penny.

Fast-forward to June 2013 where I stumbled upon an article in a broadsheet that made me think back to that hot day in Kilmarnock.[1] The article pointed out that, although Americans spend more on medicine than any nation on earth, there are an estimated 50 million with no health insurance. The reasons for this are many, but most often it is because people are unable to afford the coverage premiums. As a result, in 2009, the LA Forum, an arena more typically associated with Madonna's concerts, was transformed for eight days into a huge field hospital. That's right — a field hospital. Now, when you think of one of the most powerful countries on earth, you would assume that their field hospitals would be in Iraq or wherever their soldiers are. But no. This field hospital was in Los Angeles.

In America, the offer of free health care is so rare, and so desperately sought, that news of the medical miracle spread rapidly and there were long lines of prospective patients waiting for a whole range of medical procedures that we in the UK take for granted. This is because we have the NHS, an organization held up by some US Republicans as an evil, Orwellian attack on the right of people to enjoy the benefits of deep vein thrombosis without bloody socialists trying to interfere. This extraordinary field hospital in Inglewood, California, stood as a stark reminder that privatized health care in the West may not be all that it is made out to be. In the first two days at the LA Forum, more than 1,500 men, women and children received free treatments worth $503,000 (approximately £304,000); thirty dentists pulled 471 teeth; 320 people were given standard-issue spectacles; eighty had mammograms; dozens more had acupuncture, or saw kidney specialists. By the time the makeshift medical centre left town, it had dispensed $2 million worth of treatments to 10,000 patients.

Why there are no field hospitals in the UK . . . yet

It's easy to take the power of free health care for granted. To put it into context, every single item in Poundland will cost you more than a same-day consultation with a vastly experienced health professional who can, through their expertise, put you on a path that will hopefully stop you hurting/ dying/feeling thoroughly bloody miserable. Even those little hand fans that look like helicopters, and are only useful for amusing yourself by pretending to push them into people's faces by mistake, cost more than one of these consultations. So do the stacks of David Blaine toilet roll that allow one visit to the loo before you find yourself staring at a brown cardboard cylinder in confusion. So do the dodgy twelve-packs of batteries that run out of charge just by looking at your electrical appliance. An NHS consultation is cheaper even than the multi-packs of faux-Space Raiders where each bag contains three crisp aliens who look like they came from a planet where only the very deformed are allowed to apply for the space service. That's right — it's cheaper than all of those because it doesn't cost us anything.

So surely, then, everyone is on board with the idea of a free national health service? A service where, if you rock up ill at a hospital or at a general practice, you know for sure that the one single thing that the person who is treating you has on their mind is giving you the best treatment that they can; the most appropriate attention that you could receive. Surely everyone agrees that a publicly funded national health service is one of the crowning glories of a modern civilized society? A society that ensures that people's basic health needs are met, not based on who they are, how much they have or what job they have, but just because they are human beings.

Well, it turns out that *not* everybody is on board with this idea. In fact, not at all. And not only in the US, where Barack Obama has horrified some voters by revealing his despicable communist roots and trying to legislate to stop people from lower and middle incomes dying of wholly preventable conditions. Even in the UK, where we have seen the benefits of publicly funded health care, there are some people, albeit a minority, who are not happy with the way that the NHS works. Not one bit. Nope, for these people the NHS represents many things but it most certainly isn't a beacon of civilized society. For these people, the NHS is an arch example of the institutions of socialism run amok. An expensive, inefficient, unnecessary drain on the public purse whose insulation from the vagaries of the free market, and the vicious competition that entails, delivers consistently low standards of health care. In short, it is outdated, unnecessary and simply not fit for purpose.

Except there is one slight flaw in this viewpoint. Well, a couple of flaws actually. A recent independent survey found that users of the NHS often expressed very high levels of satisfaction with their personal experience of the medical services. Of hospital inpatients, 92% said they were satisfied with their treatment.[2]

Ninety-two per cent? Wow!

That's pretty high. Actually, that's really, really high. That's really close to 100%. Good lord. Ninety-two out of a hundred people were satisfied. Furthermore, 87% of GP users were satisfied with their GP and 87% of hospital outpatients were satisfied with the service that they received. OK, so people seem to like it. Big deal, it's still way too expensive; think of all the money that we could save with a fully privatized NHS. Of course, we'd need the odd eight-day field hospital every now and then but no system is perfect.

Oh, hang on — a study in the *Journal of the Royal Society of Medicine* recently showed that the NHS is actually one of the most cost-effective health systems in the developed world.[3] These 'surprising' findings show the NHS saving more lives for each pound spent as a proportion of national wealth than any other country apart from Ireland over the last twenty-five years. Among the seventeen countries considered, the United States health care system, complete with impromptu field hospitals, was among the least efficient and effective. Well, I never! A health system that is organized to make maximum profit for shareholders is not as effective as one that seeks to put helping people first. I'm going to need a little sit-down after that news.

Not only was the UK cheaper, says the report, it actually saved more lives, reducing the number of adult deaths per million of the population by 3,951 a year — far better than the nearest comparable European countries. France managed 2,779 lives a year and Germany 2,395.[4] So, popular with patients, cheaper *and* saves more lives than its counterparts — God forbid we let that nightmare system continue.

Bad NHS, naughty NHS!

And so we come to the purpose of this book. We all have multiple stories of using the NHS through our lives. And while I imagine every single person who picks up this book will have had some bad experiences of using the NHS, on the whole, most people are pretty satisfied. The statistics earlier highlight this. But it is not until we start to piece these NHS lives together as one whole that we can really see what an impact this institution providing free health care at the point of delivery has had on us. That is what I hope to do here: give one example of a thirty-eight-year relationship with the NHS; an NHS life, if you will.

Now it just so happens that I am the perfect person to document a life in the NHS for a number of reasons. Firstly, I don't and never have worked for the health service. Secondly, I don't receive money from any private health care providers (a small point but one that separates me from almost 200 parliamentarians). Thirdly, I like talking about myself. Good God, do I enjoy this! Alongside cycling and thinking about novel ways to hide my man boobs, talking about myself is my favourite hobby. But more importantly, I am an average person and this is an average story. I represent all the other average stories of average people whose lives are routinely and often unnoticeably held together by the people who work in our health service. I am going to present you with one man's history and ask you to consider where someone like me would be without a health service that is free at the point of use. Why? Because it is necessary. We live in a culture where the NHS is regularly and disproportionately savaged. Our media is generally disinterested in stories of good, sensitive and empathic treatment and unparalleled professionalism because they don't make engaging headlines. You are unlikely to find too many papers with the following splashed across the front pages:

'Shock finding — man who gets shoulder fixed in hospital says it all went well'

'Scandal as woman, 49, gets offered a cup of tea while she waits for her results'

'Local doctor correctly diagnoses piles'

'Disgrace as local man has to wait 7 minutes for his blood test (and then gets a really friendly nurse)'

So, instead you are going to find them here in this book. Two of the criticisms that one keeps hearing about the NHS are that a) it is inefficient, (that is, you could achieve much more by paying much less through reorganizing it) and b) it is subsumed in a morass of low standards. It is for this second reason that I am going to introduce a range of first-person accounts of why the NHS is actually, on the whole, pretty great. To help me do this I am going to introduce a largely needless and completely unscientific rating system that addresses these claims of inefficiency and low standards. The Carl Walker 'Is the NHS a bit shit or not?' system works as follows. I outline a personal health encounter and try to makes sense of whether it was a bit shit or not. Granted, this system is a little bit rough and ready and probably wouldn't excite Stephen Hawking in its complexity, but I think it will probably do the job. I do this by focusing on the following six factors:

- How long did I have to wait?
- Was I diagnosed correctly?
- Was the outcome successful?
- Did I receive sympathetic and professional health care?
- Did I spot these much-vaunted signs of

inefficiency and poor standards?
- What would the *Daily Mail* headline be for this encounter?

Through this, I hope to show that the NHS is one of the great inventions of modern times, right up there with the internet, manned flight and stuffed-crust pizza.

The ambulance

As I lay on the tarmac, with the most crushing pain in my battered right leg, I did my usual accident paralysis check. Toes and feet were moving. Excellent, I was going to walk again. Looking down at my leg I was then struck by the depressing revelation that, despite all those thousands of training miles over the winter, my season was over. I knew this because, as I looked down, I had a substantial hole in my knee through which I could see my bone — a bone, I might add, which had clearly moseyed its way across to the right by about an inch or two. I was in the middle of a busy road too, but all the traffic seemed to have stopped, so that particular concern was put to one side for the time being. The driver of the car, complete with smashed windscreen, had skidded to a halt on the central reservation and was shaking behind the wheel as if she was auditioning (quite well) for the new DVLA 'Think Bike' television advert.

A bystander had come over to repeatedly tell me, 'You just bounced off the fucking windscreen, man!' He looked like he was in shock, too. 'Like a rag doll, man, like a fucking rag doll!' I thanked him for his observation. The driver had finished her 'Think Bike' audition and came over to inspect the damage. She was clearly very distressed. She apologized profusely and repeatedly told me that she hadn't seen me. My new friend now had someone else to share his observation with so he told the driver that 'he was like a fucking rag doll, love, a rag doll!' As the rag doll had smashed her windscreen with his head, I think she was probably already privy to this information, but she was content to let him have his fun. She looked genuinely distressed and so I tried to console her. Well, as much as a man rolling around on the ground with a hole in his leg can console anyone. 'Don't worry, there's no harm done,' I lied, looking at my bike, which now looked like a drunk John Goodman had ridden it round a BMX track.

It was then that the ambulance crew arrived on the scene and went through their 'he was like a fucking rag doll' initiation ceremony. They told everyone to stand back. This was a good thing as the driver repeating her 'Think Bike' impression and the rag doll man were beginning to grate a little. I asked the ambulance men how my leg looked as I was now lying prone with my head next to my once beautiful bike.

'Oh, not so bad. You'll need an X-ray, though; it might be broken.'

'How big is the hole?' I asked as they lifted me by stretcher into the ambulance. I was pretending not to be squeamish. I told myself to think about Carl Weathers' character in *Predator*. He lost his arm and barely even noticed. Although to be fair he was fighting a seven-foot-tall monster from another planet at the time so he had plenty to distract himself with. I was just lying in an ambulance.

'Ah, probably about a 50p coin, maybe.' His more senior colleague, feeling like this initial appraisal may have had an unnecessarily negative effect on me, chipped in with, 'Nah, not a 50p — more like a 10p, I'd say.' I pointed out that there wasn't really much difference in sizes between the coins these days. The old 50p was a different matter, but these days it's only the shape that differentiates them. 'I suppose so,' the senior colleague reflected.

'Is your back or your neck hurt?' the junior colleague asked.

'Nah, it's fine, but my arse is killing me.'

'Right,' he replied with a little disappointment since, clearly, this piece of information wasn't going to help him figure out whether I needed a neck brace or not.

'Not my arsehole, my cheek!' (I had lost the skin) I added for no good reason that I could think of.

'Right.'

'Er, yup. Neck and back fine, though.'

As I sat in the back of the ambulance the paramedic asked if I wanted to call anyone, perhaps someone who might be expecting me back. Good point. I lived with my now-wife and picked up my phone to start dialling. The paramedic interrupted me to give me a little coaching. He said that in his experience there were good ways (and less good ways) to call relatives from ambulances so that you didn't scare the shit out of them. He told me not to start with the fact that I was in an ambulance but to say that I had had an accident but that I was absolutely fine, and had just hurt my leg. I tried to hide that I felt a little put out at his minimizing my gaping hole as 'just hurt my leg' when I once again remembered Carl Weathers, one arm ripped off but still firing his gun with the other. He was right. Carl Weathers would have been appalled at that kind of reaction.

'So shall I not tell her that I'm in an ambulance?'

'No, you can tell her that, just don't start with it. Do the reassuring first. Remember, start off with 'I'm fine'.'

The phone rang and when Ruth picked up all his good work just flew out of a hatch that someone had obviously left open in my brain. 'Hi, Ruthie, I'm in an ambulance and I've been hit by a car.' I looked round, the ambulance man was shaking his head in disappointment. 'It wasn't a very big car, though,' I chipped in, suddenly remembering the whole reassurance vibe. He was now looking at me like I was a dog with learning difficulties. He mouthed, 'I'm fine; just a cut leg' and so I repeated it, but in terms of immediate shock and worry the damage had been done already.

The ambulance was about to move. I asked the paramedic about the bike, about where we were going to store it. He told me that policy was that he couldn't bring the bike with us in the ambulance. It was OK though because he had found some bloke who would keep the bike for me until I could collect it. 'You've found a complete stranger who'll take

17

my £1,500 carbon-fibre racing bike? What a trooper. Wow, where do I celebrate that news?' I could have taken the bike to any town centre in Britain, left it unlocked and found just such a Samaritan in a few minutes. I moaned about it for a bit. He sympathized but ultimately he stonewalled me with the policy argument. It would have to stay with a local from the Redhill region for the time being. I crossed my fingers that he was a churchgoer. They don't normally nick things.

As we were on the way to hospital I was feeling a bit unwell so to take my mind off things I asked him how it looked.

'Well, they'll need to clean it up as you've got little bits of what looks like metal in the wound. They'll need to suture it, too, but if nothing is broken you might get away with being out later today. All depends.'

'Did you say 'metal?'' I asked, suddenly animated.

'Yes, looks like it.'

I gulped. 'You mean like Wolverine?'

'Who?'

'You know, the guy with the claws and sideburns from the *X-Men* movies?' (It turned out he had seen the movies and found this wholly inappropriate comparison amusing.) 'I'm a bit like Wolverine's shorter, fatter brother.'

'I'm not sure you can compare a mutant with metal spikes in his fists to a bloke who has picked up a few tiny scraps of metal in a leg wound.' It was a good point and it's not like I had much of a backstory. Comic book characters get bitten by spiders or zapped by radiation or struck by lightning in order to develop their superpowers. They tend not to pick up debris from the roads following very minor accidents on their push-bikes. 'Should I call ahead and tell them that Wolverine is coming?' he joked. At this, we both laughed and, for a few seconds, I forgot about the searing pain in my leg and the nausea building in my stomach.

Following my X-rays and stitches, wound-cleaning and bandaging, I was just about ready to go home. Ruth came down to pick me up and told me that she had managed to squeeze the bike into the back of the car. Turns out the ambulance crew had dropped it off.

Length of wait
Ambulance was there in no time; certainly under ten minutes. Even as I lay crumpled on the floor bitching about my newly perforated knee I had time to reflect on how impressive this was.

Gregory House index (diagnostic capacity)

They managed to successfully diagnose that I wasn't Wolverine. That said, I won't give too much praise for this act of medical sleuthing since I look more like the outcome of an experiment to see if Phil Mitchell's head could survive on Danny Devito's body.

Successful outcome?

I got to the hospital and my bike got to the hospital too. So yes, I would have taken that at the start.

Sympathetic and professional health care?

I got a free coaching session on how to tell relatives about the accident (which I ignored), they bent the rules to take my bike, and let me down gently over my Wolverine pretensions. I really couldn't complain.

Any signs of inefficiency and poor standards?

Nope. They got there in under ten minutes and they were attentive, sensitive, and humoured the excesses of my vanity. And they went out of their way to accommodate me (and my bike). The only poor standards that day were shown by the car driver who decided to play a game of 'exit the junction with my eyes closed'.

Front page headline you won't find in the *Daily Mail*
'Ambulance crew are really nice to Wolverine after he gets hit by a car.'

The posh doctor

Now, this example is a little different from the rest because I'm not entirely sure where the doctor came from. I went to university at Royal Holloway College and this particular example of care came at a doctor's clinic on the campus. I understand that the doctor was an NHS doctor and just dropped in to carry out regular clinics on campus but, for reasons that are about to be explained, this was difficult to know.

Anyway, I was in my third year at university and I noticed a rash appear down below. When a man spots a rash down below the first thought that goes through his brain — even before 'I wonder what that rash on my genitals is?' — usually goes something like: 'I'm going to have to have another man touch my groin'. That this man will be a medical

21

practitioner doesn't really serve to soften the blow.

Of course, at first it was very small (the rash), less than a centimetre, and so I told myself that it was probably just a passing rash. Having a long-term girlfriend at another university and being the faithful type, I didn't expect it to be an STD. That, however, didn't stop me going to the library to get books on different venereal diseases in order to reassure myself. Now to this day I maintain that no human being should have to encounter some of the images that I witnessed in that book. By God, it was painful to read. To make matters worse, a girl from my course sidled up behind me and saw me engrossed by these pictures of swollen, bloodied, pus-filled genitals. As our course was biology it was not impossible that my interest in this topic was driven by my degree, but the look on her face betrayed the fact that she thought I had VD. 'What module are you doing that for?' Shit. Now I was in trouble since, to the best of my knowledge, we didn't have a 'Rotting Cocks 101' module. My mind scanned quickly through my chosen courses to think of one that might include the necessity of looking at pictures of diseased penises. Nothing sprang to mind so I mumbled 'genetics' weakly and looked away.

Anyway, the good news was that my penis didn't look like any of the ones in the book. The bad news was that someone I barely knew assumed that I had VD and might very well be sharing the revelation to fellow course-mates. So I waited a few days for it to clear up. The only problem was that, not only did it not clear up, it got gradually worse. There was nothing else for it. I'd have to go and get myself checked out.

Waiting nervously in the waiting room I rehearsed how I was going to introduce my genitals to the doctor. I wondered whether there might be a way of getting the cream that I needed without actually exposing my groin to public display. Perhaps he would just let me describe the rash and then move on? Of course, deep down I knew that getting groin cream without an examination would be like getting your MOT without showing the mechanic your car: impossible. So when my name was called I took a deep breath and headed for the treatment room.

As I walked in, a new and unexpected challenge struck me and it was one that was going to complicate this encounter. My doctor, a middle-aged man, was quite literally the poshest-sounding person that I had ever come across. He was so posh that his voice sounded like he was parodying posh people.

If it wasn't for the fact that I kept picking up the word 'penis,' I might have been none the wiser that he was the doctor. He introduced himself but I misheard his name — unless, of course, his name was 'Dr Goat'. I suppose this was possible.

Anyway, through hand gestures Dr Goat managed to make it clear that he wanted to see my penis. I delayed slightly just in case he should suddenly change his mind and belatedly realize that he could diagnose my groin rash without looking at it after all. No such luck. I undid my belt and let my trousers and boxers fall to the floor. Dr Goat muttered something to the effect that it would have been sufficient just to take my penis out without letting all clothes fall to the floor. He had the countenance of a man who had waded through more VD than he could shake a stick at (if, indeed, shaking a stick at VD were possible). I suddenly became conscious that I looked more like a man preparing for a blow job than one waiting for a medical inspection. I found myself mumbling, 'It isn't from . . . ' My intention was to let him know that it wasn't VD but I couldn't think of an appropriate word for sex. After all, Dr Goat made Hugh Grant sound like Chas and Dave, so I couldn't exactly say 'fucking' or 'shagging'. I found myself finishing the sentence with the word ' . . . intercourse'. Aware that this word is only used in Christian sex education videos, I then corrected it with 'sex'.

Dr Goat shot me an 'I'll decide on that' look and then pulled a chair up so that his face was about two inches from my groin. I heard him mutter the word 'testicles'. However, the problem in this instance did not concern my testicles and this was something I was keen to impart to the doctor. On receipt of this information Dr Goat suddenly and with atypical clarity said, 'That's the thing about testicles — they are funny creatures.' I found this statement surprising because it was the first thing I could understand, and it led me to reflect that maybe he had an unusual and debilitating disorder that only allowed him to talk clearly if he was talking about testicles. I found my mind drifting away to consider what the life of such a man would actually look like, having to find inventive ways to sneak the word 'testicles' into every sentence that you wished to communicate. I was wrenched from my musings by his repeating the last part of his sentence, 'funny creatures, indeed'. Now I won't lie, at no point in my life had I ever really thought that balls were in any sense funny but I felt a little under pressure to agree here and found myself supportively saying, 'Yes, they are, really.' I mean, on reflection, I suppose that as human body parts go they do look a little curious, but I wouldn't have paid to see them do stand up.

I had not expected much from this consultation, but the absolute minimum was a curtain to protect my modesty. Not only was there no curtain but we were stood in a room that was adjoining two others and that seemed to have a steady stream of nurses walking through whenever the mood took them. As I stood there sheepishly with my trousers round my ankles nodding 'hello' to passing nurses, I had an intriguing and not entirely welcome insight into the life of an opportunist sex pest. I had a choice at this juncture either to complain and ask for a private space for the consultation, or just silently implore the passing nurses with my eyes to get the hell out. Being British I chose the latter.

I was struck by the thought that I didn't know what to do with the rest of my body while Dr Goat closely inspected my penis. I found myself trying a number of poses including hands on hips, arms folded in front of me, casually scratching my head as if to say 'whatever, no big deal' to the steady stream of nurses passing by. In the end, I settled for hands straight down by my sides, tapping a rhythm casually on my leg. Halfway through the inspection, a nurse came over with a query for Dr Goat about another patient. So, as he talked with his nurse (who seemed to understand Goatese), I just stood there with my penis and balls out, tapping a rhythm away on my leg. Apparently, the nurse confirmed, there was a fellow student who believed that he had a fishbone stuck in his throat. While I was inclined to offer my advice that we let the fucker choke and get back to sorting my penis out, I thought better of it. Dr Goat muttered a few things and shook his head sombrely. He then turned back to me and said that I had 'jock rash' — something people often get from playing sport, apparently.

He gave me an anti-fungal cream prescription and then told me that I shouldn't masturbate for a while. At least I was pretty sure that was what he said. The problem was that he delivered this advice with a laugh of resigned futility, as if he was giving the advice to a chronic masturbator, one whose addiction to choking the bishop was so extreme that he could never stop, even if he wanted to. Which I thought was unfair. I made a point of telling him that not masturbating wouldn't be a problem. He then looked really confused. So much so that it was clear that, whatever he had said to me, it obviously wasn't 'Don't masturbate'. I then ran out and went home to bed.

Length of wait
Fifteen to twenty minutes. Nowhere near long enough bearing in mind what was about to come.

Gregory House index (diagnostic capacity)
Hard to say how difficult it is to diagnose jock rash. I'll give him the benefit of the doubt either way because he got it spot on.

Successful outcome?
Yes, two useful outcomes. A correct diagnosis meant that my rash was clear in a few days. I also learned that you will never see a more confused face on another human being than by telling them out of the blue that you wouldn't have a problem abstaining from masturbation.

Sympathetic and professional health care?
Couldn't understand a word he was saying but he was nice enough and tried his best (as much as is possible for a man who could only

achieve clarity if a sentence had 'testicle' in it) to be reassuring and gentle.

Any signs of inefficiency and poor standards?
He could have fished out a curtain if I'm being picky but it was pretty good.

Front page heading you won't find in the *Daily Mail*
'Confusion reigns in Goatese consultation.'

The daddy nappy challenge

Most people tend to take up pretty conventional hobbies. Things like horse riding, or stamp collecting or maybe a little bit of genealogy where intrepid amateur historians, through hard work and painstaking research, are able uncover that their distant ancestors were just as uninteresting as they are. There are, however, more unconventional hobbies that some people engage in. For instance, some people enjoy taxidermy, magic or inline skating. To this list I would cautiously add the pastime of 'slagging off nurses'.

Whenever there appears to be a crisis or a difficulty in the NHS, the incumbent health secretary is faced with a difficult decision. They have the choice either to:

a) accept that a prolonged underfunding of the service had contributed to an economic, cultural and occupational environment in which the present crisis took form, and understand that only a sustained attempt to increase financial support could really begin to address the symptoms of this structural issue

or

b) slag off some nurses

For those who decide that option *b* is the most appropriate, the next step is to figure out, with the help of special advisors, the best way to do it.

Political Toady: 'Minister, we need to react to this fast. Early word says the Walker Report makes a number of criticisms of A&E waiting times as well as the number of beds available in the South West in the last twelve months.'

Minister: 'Bugger. This isn't good.

I've only been in this role for six months and can't have this pinned to my back. Can we dust off the old 'The Royal College of Nursing are more concerned about their members than patients and nurses aren't prepared to do menial tasks anymore because they are too busy sitting around smoking fags and planning expensive foreign holidays' one?'

Political Toady: 'I was going to suggest the very same. Might be worth spicing it up; suggest that it is now entrenched nursing practice for nurses to slap patients across the face for even so much as looking at them.'

Minister: 'Yes, yes, excellent.'

Political Toady: 'On an unrelated matter, in your Channel 4 news interview later they might ask about the government's U-turn on wind farms, so be ready for that.'

Minister: 'Can we pin that on the

nurses, too?'
Political Toady: 'Fuck it, why not.'

I'm left a little bit confused about this. In my own personal experience, compassion and a willingness to get their hands dirty are the two qualities that have pretty much characterized every interaction I have ever had with nurses. Of course, it's possible that I have just been unusually lucky and used hospital services on the days when the lazy, fag-smoking, foreign-holiday-buying nurses are having their day off from slapping patients in the face. But I don't think so. I could reel off a range of examples of this compassion, but the first that springs to mind occurred just after our daughter was born.

Following the birth I went home for a few hours' sleep before returning in the morning. When I came back I was faced with what I will refer to as the 'daddy nappy challenge'. For the uninitiated, when you walk into the postnatal ward, your wife and child are usually there with a whole bunch of other new mother/baby combinations. In our case there were eight beds on the ward and a variety of profoundly awkward-looking new dads looking up vasectomy clinics on their smartphones as they tried to get their newborns to stop screaming in their ears. When you enter this arena one thing becomes immediately obvious: it is now *your* shift. Mums have been through the carnage of childbirth, have most likely been up all night tending to their child and are unable to sleep owing to pain/the crying of other babies on the ward/changing their newborn's nappy/feeding, etc. As you walk in there, all bright and breezy the morning after, everything about that arena screams: 'Right, your turn!' And rightly so.

The first of these challenges is the 'daddy nappy challenge'. Sooner or later your newborn is going to shit itself. Now you have three options here:

a) You let your wife go off and do it.
b) You let the nurses do it (and health secretaries through history would be amazed to discover that nurses routinely do this to help mums try to get some sleep and recover).
c) *You* do it.

These choices can be simplified to:

a) You look selfish.
b) You look pathetic.
c) You don't look selfish or pathetic.

When my turn came, a nurse came over and kindly asked if I'd like her to do this one. I thanked her for the offer but, summoning an absolutely unwarranted bravado, told her that I was absolutely fine to do it. This pleased the nurse and, I suspect, placed me on the 'marginally less useless new dad' list that my imagination suggested they were compiling in their nurses' station at the entrance to the ward. The problem was, of course, that I *was* useless. I really, really was. I had never — and some might think this odd bearing in mind the nine-month planning phase at my disposal — given a single bit of thought as to how one might change a nappy. It's not that I hadn't intended to do them; indeed, I *had*. I suspect, though, that I had thought it was so easy that it didn't actually require any thought. This might account for why, during the session on 'changing a nappy' in the day-long class on parenting at the local hospital, I was more interested in making smart-arse comments about the beard of one of the fellow impending parents to my bored wife. Now was the time of his revenge. He may have had a beard that made him look like a Victorian pederast, but he knew how to do a nappy and I didn't.

I was told that some of the dads in the ward had bottled it and this set me up a treat.

If I could get out, change the nappy and come back in then it would be garlands and compliments ahoy from nurses and patients alike. I could moonwalk back into the wards bathed in my 'new man' status. The problem was that I suddenly felt like Ted Danson in *Three Men and a Baby*. And I didn't have Tom Selleck around to pick up the pieces for me. Christ, I didn't even have a Steve Guttenberg. As I wheeled my daughter's transparent little plastic bucket toward the changing station, I realized I had about fifteen seconds to figure this out — twenty if I walked *really* slowly. 'Think, think, think,' I implored myself. I got my phone out to see if I could google 'doing a newborn's nappy'.

Shit, no signal.

As I entered the changing station I looked around the walls. Perhaps someone had left a point by point diagram on the wall of how to do a nappy? No luck; all that was on the walls was a load of useless shit about resuscitation equipment. Unfortunately, there also were three women already in there. One was changing her newborn's nappy and the other two were chatting to her and cradling their own little miniature malcontents.

'Don't be Ted Danson, be Tom Selleck,' I repeatedly and silently begged myself as I pushed Anna into a corner of the room. I may even have been saying it out loud, as the mothers gave me a look of concerned pity. At this point, one of the nurses came in pretending to be getting something, but I suspect she was there to check that I hadn't put the nappy on my daughter's head. Or at least that's what my paranoia was telling me. It may actually have been that the whole of the ward didn't revolve around my immediate trauma and that she did really have something to collect. Either way, she gave me a smile that said, 'The offer is still on the table,' but I was in too deep now.

'Make sure you do it nice and tight,' she offered helpfully on the way out. This was useful as I had at that point been considering that very aspect. I got my kit ready and cracked my knuckles a few times. I had a look out of the corner of my eye to watch how the other woman, who was now on her own, was doing it, but when she looked up and saw me looking at her, it all felt a little creepy; as though I had borrowed a child so that I could go and hit on a woman who had just given birth.

As I took the nappy off I was faced by what I can only describe as a barrel-load of korma flooding everywhere. I panicked and closed it back up. My daughter was only one day old but her face betrayed a look of genuine disappointment. I suppose it's good that she gets into the habit of being disappointed early, I thought to myself — it'll only be harder if it hits her later. OK, a deep breath, and I went back in. If this was going to work it would have to be quick. The problem this time was that I spotted the stump of the umbilical cord, a sight that made it straight into the top ten list of the grimmest things I've ever seen. It was black and rotten (apparently normal) and I was transfixed by it as the contents of the open nappy started to break their boundaries. I came back to life just in time. I got rid of the old nappy, put on the new one and spent about three hours trying to figure out how tight to make it. I didn't want her leaking in the night. I was representing more than myself here; I was representing new men everywhere. I had to demonstrate competence. At the same time, I didn't want it so tight that she started turning blue. So I tried various measures of tightness — about twenty-five or so. I took my phone out and quickly googled 'baby suffocate tight nappy'. This didn't help. A whole load of articles came up about babies suffocating and how dangerous tight nappies were. I took a guess. I decided from nowhere that if I could put two fingers between nappy and belly without them feeling like they were being throttled then it would be OK. I've stuck with the two fingers test ever since, even though it has absolutely no basis in scientific fact.

I then fumbled forever, trying to match the poppers on her babygrow, ditched the korma, and sauntered out of the changing room like it was all no big deal. 'Hey, well done, you!' one of the passing nurses said as she walked by. I shot her a look like the Fonz used to give in *Happy Days* when he was being particularly cool. 'Nothing to it,' I lied and then delivered my daughter back to my wife, feeling for all the world that I was developing PTSD.

I can't speak highly enough of the nurses who staffed the post-natal c-section ward in Worthing Hospital. They were superb. They were patient, reassuring and conscientious. Much has been made of the modern-day nurse feeling too important to get involved in some of the more elementary aspects of patients' care, but this lot were always tidying, cleaning up, coming over for informal chats, checking if things were OK, asking if we needed anything, and taking people to the toilets (patients, that is; nobody tried to take *me* to the toilet). I'm not one who gets particularly excited about leaving my ill wife and child in a ward full of strangers, but with these nurses around I felt unusually secure.

And when I took my daughter for little walks around the ward, which I must have traversed around 500 times in the two days that we were there, they were always friendly, smiling, asking how things were and making people feel really at home.

Length of wait
When Anna's nappy turned into a code-red situation, the nurses were on hand almost immediately to offer help. And they were still there when I emerged from the changing station just before Anna's first birthday.

Gregory House index (diagnostic capacity)
The nurses correctly diagnosed that I didn't know my arse from my elbow and subtly tried to help me out.

Successful outcome?
Well, the nappy wasn't on Anna's head and it wasn't on me so I have to tentatively conclude that it was a success.

Sympathetic and professional health care?
Superb. They even managed not to show any visible disdain for dads who opted out of the nappy challenge (apart from one who said he

couldn't do it because of a sore shoulder; they looked at him as if he had just announced with a wink that he wasn't wearing any underwear).

Any signs of inefficiency and poor standards?
None. They were visibly rushed off their feet but maintained a level of care that was deeply impressive.

Front page heading you won't find in the *Daily Mail*
'Conscientious nurse comes to the rescue, after realizing that the Fonz doesn't have a clue how to change a nappy.'

'Lifted'

As we were being shown around the hospital in preparation for the birth of my daughter, I remember allowing myself a little chuckle when one of my group asked whether it would be OK to bring in some music to play for when her child was being born. This struck me as a deeply flawed piece of thinking. If I think back to the kind of shit that my dad used to play when I was a child, there wasn't a single record of his that I

40

would have liked to accompany my passage into this world. The trauma of birth, of being wrenched from a lovely, warm cocoon that has been your home for nine months, of being half-drowned as you are forced to breathe for yourself for the first time and suddenly being exposed to what feels like sub-zero temperatures, was not going to be improved by suddenly being hit by some Neil Sedaka or Johnny Mathis.

I was reminded of this thought when my son came along. He was born by planned Caesarean, a process that had been, up until the day, handled exquisitely by all members of the medical staff involved. I couldn't believe just how relaxing and agreeable the process was. Our delivery team were friendly and jovial and talked us through each stage of the process in advance of us going into theatre. As I put on my gown I could just make out the distant sound of music. It was Mark Morrison's 'Return of the Mack'.

For those who don't remember Morrison, he was an R&B one-hit wonder in the 1990s who fancied himself as the UK's answer to Tupac. However, instead of shooting people, he got caught and prosecuted for sending someone who looked nothing like him to do his community service for him. I recall thinking to myself that hospitals are tough enough places without someone introducing Leicester's premier bad boy into the mix. The problem was that it was getting louder the closer I got to theatre. Sure enough, as I walked into theatre, I made the devastating discovery that *our* theatre, the site of my son's impending birth, was the source of the music.

And this wasn't the worst of it. Our consultant, the man who had talked us through the process, who had been so reassuring and competent and responsive in the lead-up to the birth, was tapping his feet. And it wasn't just a casual tapping of the feet that one does to the rhythm of some background music. It was an 'I fucking love the Mack' tapping of the feet, accompanied by head nodding and shaking. I spotted the offending radio in the corner of the room. Good God, I was placing my child's life in the hands of a Mark Morrison fan.

I was faced with a dilemma. Either I could ask for the radio to be turned off, and risk taking away a device that was relaxing the consultant who was delivering my child, or I could leave it on and have my son born to a really shit song. 'Is it OK if we have the radio on?' the doctor asked considerately. 'Yeah, of course,' I lied. My wife was busy thinking about having her stomach cut open and so Mark Morrison wasn't such a pressing issue for her at that time. As it was the radio I told myself that we might strike it lucky and have some decent music just at the point of birth.

'OK, if you need anything at all or if you feel any pain, just let me know,' the consultant said to my wife. 'And Carl, it's probably worth you staying that side of the screen if you don't like blood.' I didn't really take heed of this warning because Simply Red had just come on the radio. This was bad. The thought of having to sit my son down later in his life to explain that Mick Hucknall sang him into life was unbearable. I needed something to take my mind off his crooning about falling from the stars, so I started to think about things I'd rather confess to my son in later life than that he was born to Simply Red. In the time that the song was on I managed to come up with the following:

- that he was adopted
- that I had a conviction for flashing
- that I video people while they use the toilet
- that Sting thinks I'm pretentious
- that I was Simon Cowell's hairdresser
- that I once buggered a dog for a bet

And then it stopped. Thank God! I could

relax. Or at least I thought I could until Craig David reared his ugly head. By this point I had got it into my head that it actually mattered. That because of some superstition beyond my understanding, the song might have some bearing on who he would end up being, like a mystical harbinger of the future. As Craig David's voice floated across the operating theatre it struck me that my son might have a really shit pencil beard and talk endlessly about sexing up a lady all week before chilling on a Sunday.

'Well done, you're both doing really well,' a nurse came over to reassure us. Since Ruth had been given an epidural and I was just sitting there trying not to look at the business end, I wasn't sure that the praise was deserved, but it was nice of her anyway. Even though I was being tortured by a series of musical mediocrities that might eventually come to define my son's life, I had time to note how amazing it was to watch this medical team go about their work. Supremely coordinated and organized, even with a young life literally in their hands, they still managed to keep us engaged as part of the process.

As Craig David made a welcome exit I lost concentration and found myself peeping behind the long piece of cloth that constituted the makeshift barrier. What I saw was a little bit like the John Hurt stomach scene in the first *Alien* film, except without the alien. Ruth must have caught this and asked what I saw. I couldn't answer her as I was pretty concentrated on not throwing up in my mouth, so I just nodded. I made a mental note to myself not ever to do that again.

'It's so funny, how we don't talk any more.' Shit, it was Cliff. No, Cliff, it's not *funny*. And nor will it be funny if my boy turns out to be a Christian tennis fan who looks like he's from a planet where people are made exclusively from old brown leather coats. What if he wears jackets with the sleeves rolled up? Shit, what if, with his jacket sleeves rolled up, my son makes it his life's ambition to destroy the Christmas charts with abominable songs? No, this is no good at all. Take your time, Andrew; hang on in there, son; there's no hurry.

The medical team and anaesthetist were carefully checking Ruth for any potential pain or discomfort. Quite ironic considering that they had just played us Simply Red, Craig David and Cliff Richard. Of course she's in pain. What next — Ronan Keating? And sure enough, Ronan Keating started to tear his way through a country and western number with all the panache of an abattoir worker wrestling an oily pig. OK, this was too far.

Alarmed, I looked at the doctor, as if he would share my obvious realization that something had to be done about this. Of course, he was in the middle of a complex operation so we weren't on the same wavelength. I mulled it over. Was it ethically acceptable to interrupt an operation to bring my son into the world to request that we change the radio station because I was worried that if he was born to a Ronan Keating song it would damage him just as surely as oxygen debt?

I shared my anxiety with my wife who, not unreasonably, also had other things on her mind at that point, primarily because she had someone else's hands inside her. Because of this she was less concerned about the impact that the most dangerous Irishman since Daniel O'Donnell might have on our son. I was on my own here. But this didn't mean that I was willing to give up. I did a little impromptu maths and figured that if I stretched my legs under the table I could wrap my foot around the cable and pull the stereo down. Now this wasn't a desired course of action by any means, but I was prepared to do it if it meant that the first voice my son heard in the world wasn't Mr Keating's.

'How long to go?' I asked one of the

nurses. She mistook this anxiety over Ireland's serial songslayer for a general anxiety about the process. She came over and talked us through what had happened so far, how well it was going, how well we were doing and what still had to happen. Bless her, she was really lovely. My eyes were screaming 'Please make this hell end,' but not for the reasons she was thinking. The most important thing was that she had said fifteen to twenty minutes to go. Not even Ronan's greatest masterpieces lasted that long.

Of course, Ronan was followed by a Sting number. Sting is possibly the only man out of the 7 billion people on earth who would have me pining for Ronan Keating. As Sting lumbered his way through an eviscerating five minutes I wondered whether my son was destined to boast about his sex life to disinterested people and save turtles. A quick look over (although not that far over) to my wife confirmed that things were not yet at the endgame, so I relaxed a little and tried to figure out whether the radio had been tuned to Guantanamo Bay FM.

Then a Muse track came on. I knew it was Muse because it sounded like Radiohead after a series of debilitating strokes. Now this really wasn't good. The medical team were starting to prepare us for the birth and all I could think of was that if my son was born to a Muse song he would, in all likelihood, be an adult bedwetter. And I'd have to apologize to him every day of his life.

'Dad, I'm twenty-two and still pissing the bed.'

'I know, son; it's my fault. Muse were playing when you were born. You won't remember them, but if there had been a music industry competition for bedwetting, they would have walked away with it. I'm sorry, son. I let you down.'

And then it segued into 'Lifted' by the Lighthouse Family. For those not familiar with the Lighthouse Family, the band comprised two men who appeared to have devoted their adult professional lives to writing tunes that would excite estate agents. And so it was that on 19 August 2011 (not that you'd ever guess it, given the song choices of the DJ) my little estate agent was brought into the world. The only child in history to be born covering his ears with his hands.

What I have thus far neglected to emphasize properly is how remarkably easy the whole process was for Ruth and me. The operation was relaxed, with the surgeon talking to us all the way through it, telling us how well it was going. It had all the urgency of three pensioners doing a jigsaw. What made it so relaxing for us was not just how calm and in control the surgical team clearly were, but that they regularly took the time to tell us what they were doing, how they were doing it and, of course, that everything was going well. In fact, it had gone so well that what should have been an anxiety-ridden medical procedure went so smoothly that I had time to think about the songs on the radio.

I've even forgiven them for the Lighthouse Family. I hope Andrew will, too.

Length of wait
About an hour of Guantanamo FM.

Gregory House index (diagnostic capacity)
Not really applicable in this instance.

Successful outcome?
Yes. A beautiful baby boy. Many babies cry when they are born but there was something in my son's cry that was more than just 'Good God, it's cold out here'. His was the guttural cry that all sensible human beings make when hearing the Lighthouse Family for the first time.

Sympathetic and professional health care?
I know he was busy but he really should have put his foot down at Sting.

Any signs of inefficiency and poor standards?
He was tapping his feet to Mark Morrison.

Front page heading you won't find in the *Daily Mail*
'NHS surgeon who is stuck in a taste time capsule performs superb Caesarean while trying simultaneously to kill new dad.'

Is there a doctor on the plane (or tube)?

In terms of coming into contact with health professionals, being an epileptic can have some unusual consequences. Most people with chronic illnesses get to choose when and where they consult a doctor. That is, their illness flares up and then they make a decision to contact their GP. One of the more annoying features of epilepsy is that the fits don't tend to tell you when they are coming so that you can contact the neurologist (or at least a person with a nice, soft comfortable floor). Instead, fits tend to happen whenever

50

they can be arsed. And if you're unlucky it might just be the case that they happen in public. This is usually not a good thing.

One such event happened to me around ten years ago on a busy Tube train in London. I was travelling back from work on the Central Line, trying to figure out how many of the people in my carriage had legs that were long enough to stretch and touch the chairs opposite. I was trying surreptitiously to figure out how far I had to slouch down in my seat before my Ewok-sized legs would touch. ('A long way' was the answer.) My highbrow reflections were cut short rather savagely by an epileptic fit. Perhaps my brain had got bored of being used for silly thoughts and decided to rebel. Usually I get a few seconds' warning before it goes into a full meltdown and on this occasion I had time to ever-so-briefly remember that my last public fit had been in a queue of punters in Greenwich market where the fit had presumably been my brain's way of protecting me against buying a really shit jacket.

My particular brand of epilepsy is called temporal lobe epilepsy. My fits are more like blackouts and don't take the thrashing around *grand mal* form that is more commonly recognized as epilepsy. I tend to shout out random and usually unpleasant things or cry out in pain as I collapse to the floor. Mostly I am utterly oblivious to the outside world but on this occasion I was unfortunately half-sentient. Now normally fits are accompanied by complete amnesia of the time period around the fit but my neurologist at the time, who was trying to stop me having four fits a day, had asked me to write down everything I could remember immediately before and after the fit. And, being a good patient, I recorded the following events.

So I started to have a fit. An older man, who looked like a City type, looked at me for a while in puzzlement and then announced that someone should call an ambulance. Then he asked someone — I'm not sure who — 'Is he having a stroke?' Now this gentleman had obviously missed the 'how to ask a good question in the event of someone having a fit' class in primary school, as had his colleague, a commuter who looked a little bit like a fat Gene Wilder and who replied with surprising confidence that, yes, it was in fact a stroke.

Now, of course, at this point I was in no position to enlighten these gents otherwise, although I remember thinking at the time that my funny rolling about on the train floor didn't look like a stroke. Hadn't they seen the adverts where people's mouths look all funny and they go limp?

One woman piped up that she would call the driver but not before pointing out that her dad had Parkinson's and that it looked a bit like that. 'Come on, lady, not even close,' I thought, as I concentrated on trying not to dribble or bang my head. And then from the other end of the carriage bounded an odd-looking man, with the head of Rodney from *Only Fools and Horses* on a fatter, shorter body. With no little confidence he announced that he was a chiropractor. He said it with the authority of a man who felt that this fact was entirely relevant to my epileptic fit. My understanding was that chiropractors fixed peoples' backs or toes or something. Either way, it wasn't brains. However, the others in the carriage seemed reassured by this particular health professional, especially when he added that he did occupational therapy for NHS patients.

'Is he breathing?' our new Underground brain expert asked. Oh, Christ, he's going to try to resuscitate/kiss me. This was potentially worse than the fit itself. 'His mouth is moving,' said fat Gene Wilder, bending down to inspect closer but then obviously realizing that if I wasn't then he might be the one expected to administer CPR. He sat up rather sharpish as this thought flooded his grey matter. 'That doesn't mean he's breathing, though,' our chiropractor replied, showing immediately that his years of training in toes or backs was not wasted. 'We might need an open airway,' he followed up quickly. Actually you might want to leave my airway the fuck alone, I thought whilst intermittently trying not to black out. 'This is bloody typical,' came a voice from further down the carriage. Although I couldn't see the voice's owner it was clearly a woman who was bored with the daily grind of having people fit in front of her.

'I'm going to put him in the recovery position,' the chiropractor said but his authority was immediately challenged by fat Gene Wilder who noted that he'd heard that you should never try to move a stroke victim. This was turning out to be one of the most interesting and potentially worrying fits that I had ever had. 'This is definitely Parkinson's,' piped the Parkinson's woman before our chiropractor pointed out that people don't just have attacks of Parkinson's on trains. This seemed like a pretty good point to me and I was glad that he had made it. My fits usually last for around a minute and I was praying for this particular one to end before I found somebody draining blood through a hole in my head. 'Let's just hold fast,' the chiropractor said, 'he looks like he's in no immediate danger.' Aha, at last, a man talking my language. Somebody listen to him. He may be an expert on toes but he's on to something here.

Slowly the fit subsided and the agonizing fug of sensations, memories and neurological impulses withdrew their claws from my battered brain. I was then slowly able to draw a premature close to the impromptu parlour game of 'guess what's happening to the writhing chubby bloke on the floor'.

Then followed a conversation which is probably better reported verbatim:

Chiropractor:	'Relax and try to breathe slowly and deeply. You have had some kind of blackout.'
Fat Gene Wilder:	' . . . or stroke.'
Me:	'It's epilepsy; I get these fits quite a lot.'
Parkinson's woman:	'That's not epilepsy. I knew someone at school with epilepsy and they spaz out all over the place.'
Me:	'You get different types; mine is quite atypical.'
Parkinson's woman:	'I thought it was Parkinson's.'

Me:	'Yes, I know.'
Chiropractor:	'Just breathe deeply.'
Fat Gene Wilder:	'I still think it was a stroke.'
Me:	'Right, thanks.'

And there we have it. I advised my doctor the following week that I would rather not write down what happens straight afterwards in future because I found it far too stressful. Perhaps there is a protective function behind epileptics experiencing amnesia regarding their fits.

Length of wait
Not really applicable in this instance but the intervention I received from the chiropractor definitely defied the common rhetoric on the efficiency of the modern health service. I had an acute medical episode and was seen within ten to twenty seconds. It doesn't get much better than that, even if I was seen by a chiropractor in conjunction with his crack medical team of an insurance salesman and a lady who works in WHSmith.

Gregory House index (diagnostic capacity)
Well, the chiropractor knew it wasn't Parkinson's or a stroke. If nothing else he

kept any possible amateur interventions based on mythical illnesses at bay so credit where credit is due. It wasn't what you might call your typical NHS intervention but it was a health professional who moved in and kind of took over the situation. And I'm glad he did. Apart from anything else he spotted that I wasn't dead. This rather underrated piece of medical diagnosis can be very important in certain situations.

Successful outcome?
On the whole yes. A medical professional of sorts came over and even if he did not perform a specific medical intervention on me, he managed to make a couple of quite insistent members of the public *not* do things to me as if I had Parkinson's or was having a stroke. I dread to think what these interventions might have looked like.

Sympathetic and professional health care?
To be fair they all seemed rather nice and quite concerned about the stranger doing odd things on the floor of the Tube train. Apart from the lady who was barking angrily that 'this is typical,' everyone seemed interested in my plight and I found this quaintly reassuring — even if the diagnostic process itself left a

little to be desired.

Any signs of inefficiency and poor standards?
Yes, loads; but not by the one NHS staff member present.

Front page heading you won't find in the *Daily Mail*
'NHS professional uses his skills to help someone in distress in his own time. Again.'

Dealing with idiots 1: the monkey with the stethoscope

Now, granted, this example of interaction with NHS staff is a little irregular and I wasn't sure whether to include it here. However, on account of the reaction of the doctor in question I decided to do so. A few years ago, I worked as a researcher at University College London. We were doing some research on predicting episodes of depression and we needed to recruit participants to be involved in the project. Part of my role was to visit GP practices around the country to ask whether they wanted to take part in the research.

On one particular day I found myself on

the train to Devon to meet a GP and explain the project. So after a four-hour trip spent indulging my two favourite travel activities (stuffing my face with cheddar and onion McCoys and moaning about the price of cheddar and onion McCoys), I found myself rocking up to a large West Country Medical Centre.

On entry I found myself being directed to a room in the practice. It was your standard GP consulting room with various medical bits and bobs lying around. The GP had been caught up with a patient at another surgery and, while sitting with a cup of tea and some Bourbon biscuits, I found my mind wandering. I started to reflect on the impact of three packets of cheddar and onion McCoys and numerous Bourbon biscuits on an already portly man's health. As I stared in contemplation at this new opportunity to fill my belly with more unhealthy food, I was suddenly struck by the realization that I had the chance to investigate said relationship. What happened next I still have difficulty explaining properly.

There was a stethoscope sat in front of me on the desk. As the minutes ticked away and the presence of the Bourbons grew ever more intense, I started to think about picking it up and checking my heartbeat. Prominent in my mind was the fact that if the results turned out to be normal then this provided a strong rationale for me to eat these four Bourbon biscuits. However, if the stethoscope threw up negative results then I would just have to call it a day at the three packets of crisps.

Now there were two immediate problems with this scenario. The first was that I had absolutely no idea what constituted a good or bad stethoscope reading. This was less pressing than the second, which was that if I had a go at the stethoscope then a doctor would come in and I would look like a prize tool. But as much as I tried to look away, that stethoscope kept pulling me back in. I could almost hear it calling to me, 'Carl, Carl, go on, give me a try, don't worry, you won't look like a prize tool.' So I did it. I listened for any approaching feet and when I heard none I put the ear parts in my ears and the little round cold bit through my shirt and onto my chest. Well, the good news was that I could pick up my heartbeat loud and clear. This boded well on the Bourbon front. However, with a wearisome predictability the doctor that I was waiting to impress also came in at that moment and looked at me as if a macaque had somehow made it through reception and was amusing itself in her consulting room.

'Are you going to live?' she asked in a tone

normally reserved for especially stupid children. I said, 'Oh, I was just . . . ' and paused, realizing that there was no good way to finish this sentence other than ' . . . being a fucking idiot'. The least I could have done was prepare a line in case I'd got caught. I was kicking myself for this failure in advanced planning. Then I heard the following words come out of my mouth: ' . . . testing out this model of stethoscope'.

It seems that some part of my subconscious had decided that the best angle here was the 'I'm an authority on stethoscopes' approach. I've no idea why it chose this. Now, I have a special talent for immediately losing people's respect but even by my exalted standards this was quick.

'Oh, you know about stethoscopes?' she asked suspiciously. Here I had a choice, just duck out and walk away or stick with the 'stethoscope expert' angle. The only smart move here was to just 'fess up. Instead, I found myself saying, 'Yeah a bit, haven't seen one of these in a while.' My subconscious had decided to take a punt that this model was rare or unusual or even that there was some variation in stethoscopes used. 'Really? These are standard issue across the NHS now.' Bollocks, I really needed that not to be the case. Right about now I needed there to be lots of different types of stethoscopes and for doctors not to recognize one from the other. The wriggle room was rapidly decreasing. 'Ah, times change,' I said wistfully as if I, despite being a good ten years younger than this doctor, had come from a different generation of stethoscopes and was suddenly overcome by a wave of stethoscope nostalgia. I then stuffed a whole Bourbon in my mouth and waited for her to ask me to stop being a weirdo and to leave. I must have stuffed the Bourbon in with very little finesse because she then asked me if I was hungry. 'Not really. I had three packets of cheese McCoys on the way down,' I mumbled through a mouthful of Bourbon and, on noticing the disapproving look on her face, I lied — 'and an apple'.

That she didn't immediately ask me to leave was to her immense credit as she decided that this lying plebeian deserved his chance to pitch the project despite his obvious shortcomings.

Length of wait
OK, it's hard to use my usual criteria here since it wasn't a consultation *per se*. The wait was long but that's because this doctor was probably prioritizing her patients over watching an imbecile dig himself deeper and deeper into a hole.

Gregory House index (diagnostic capability)

She took little more than twenty seconds to diagnose me as a professional goon. In thirty years of medical care I have never been diagnosed with such accuracy and speed.

Successful outcome?

For me, I managed to get the Bourbon biscuits and not have to explain to my boss that the police were called to remove me from the practice. OK, my standards were obviously quite low, but still . . . For the doctor, she managed to finesse a cretin out of her consulting room without there being a scene. Everyone was a winner.

Sympathetic and professional health care?

She was lovely. Despite being consistently lied to by a strange man abusing her medical equipment, she was always polite and friendly.

Any signs of inefficiency and poor standards?

If a heroin addict came into the surgery they wouldn't have left heroin lying around. Had a suicidal person come in, they wouldn't have littered the desk with scalpels and paracetamol. I was a man with the mental age of around nine so they really had no business leaving a stethoscope within sight. Still, I suppose I couldn't have expected them to know this.

Front page heading you won't find in the *Daily Mail*
'GP nice and respectful to dickhead.'

Dr Spadehands

I have the perhaps unusual record of having had my undercarriage inspected by the medical fraternity on no less than four occasions in my life. And while I am painfully aware that this is edging toward the kind of number that might pique the interest of the local police sex pest department, I can say with absolute certainty that all four have at least been necessary. Moreover, during all four I have found my own embarrassment and self-consciousness met with a range of medical staff whose responsiveness and sensitivity were pretty remarkable. This example concerns the first time that I found a lump downstairs.

The finding of a lump on a testicle is not generally a good thing. In fact, on what would be an admittedly unusual list of things you

64

don't want to find on your testicles, it nestles comfortably between a piranha and an industrial vice. When you find what feels like a lump on your testicle the automatic impulse is to tell yourself that it is probably nothing. This is not, as many might think, an immature response of denial from a person unwilling to face up to the fragility of their own mortality. Nope, it has nothing to do with cancer whatsoever. It is simply a deep and profound desire to avoid having a stranger feel your balls. When I found myself in this position a few years ago I went through the usual two-stage medical consultation process. The first involves making an appointment with a GP and telling them your symptoms without mentioning the lump. So you rock up and tell the doctor about your dull groin and back pains in the hope that he or she will give you a nice tidy answer that doesn't involve testicular lumps.

And sometimes they will. Maybe they'll talk about stomach strains or viruses and you'll leave the surgery feeling reassured that you won't in the imminent future have a doctor touching your balls. And this is great. For about a week. And then you realize that if you got some scales out and tried to balance the inconvenience and discomfort of having a testicular examination against a slow, lingering death from undiagnosed cancer, there would be no contest. You then administer yourself a metaphorical slap in the face and find yourself rocking up for appointment two.

So there I was being ushered into the doctor's room and the first thing I noticed was a Chelsea Football Club calendar on the wall. I made a joke that I didn't want to be treated by a Chelsea fan. I had initially intended this to relax the atmosphere for my impending gonad examination. However, it dawned on me that insulting the football team of a man who is about to hold your testicles in his grip in a private place might not be up there with Edison's lightbulb moment. This was confirmed when his face suggested that my joke was as welcome as a *Family Fortunes* box set.

As I sat down on the chair it struck me for the first time in what must have been five years of visiting this doctor just what a large pair of hands he had. Good God, those were big hands; like he had a rosette at home somewhere for first place in a 'fucking big hands' competition. These bad boys were huge. There was a momentary pause as he tried to understand why I had stopped talking and was just staring at his hands.

'Are you OK, Carl?' he asked. Having

managed to peel my eyes away from the two huge slabs of ham dangling at the ends of his wrists I reassured him that I was fine. I told him why I was there. Whilst trying to maintain a veneer of professionalism I could see from a range of microfacial movements that he was about as excited about touching my balls as I was about placing them in his Incredible Hulk hands. At this point, and never having had such an examination before, I was watching his every move like a hawk. He picked up a small machine and held it briefly. It was a small metal contraption with some glass in it and a small hole. Maybe this was a testicle examination machine of some sort? I imagined that he might have to squeeze my nut in through the small hole in the top so that he could look at it through the little glass window. The problem was that the hole on top was very small. I was worried that maybe he had picked up the kiddies' version by mistake. Anyway, it turned out that this little metal box was only being picked up because it was in the way of the rubber gloves. I breathed a partial sigh of relief. Partial because I knew my nuts weren't going into that mini viewing booth. However, the whole rubber glove thing brought with it a new challenge. The doctor would now need to perform the not inconsiderable feat of finding some rubber gloves that would stretch over his by now gargantuan fingers (I think they were growing in front of me). I momentarily panicked that putting these gloves on meant that a testicle examination necessitated some kind of anal inspection too. For too many years I had watched sitcoms and sketch shows that inextricably linked rubber gloves with arseholes. And then it dawned on me that he just didn't want to touch my balls with his flesh. Which seemed fair enough.

So now he was six inches from my face and searching my balls with his hands. I figured that starting some banal conversation to cut the uncomfortable atmosphere would benefit both of us. Recalling a school friend who had a twisted testicle seemed topical and relevant so I said, 'I once had a school friend who had a twisted testicle.' The problem was that after I heard this come out of my mouth I realized that I literally didn't have a single other thing to say about it. His reply of 'Oh, right — I see' reflected that he had spotted my conversation-starter for what it was, but he decided to throw me a bone and gave me a couple of facts about twisted testicles that converted a really embarrassing utterance into a conversation. I silently thanked him for that concession. My first attempt at diversionary conversation hadn't been a rip-roaring success and had necessitated him throwing me a life raft, but it suddenly struck me that I could make it all up by joking that 'I don't normally let a man touch my balls on a first date.' A little devil on one shoulder was telling me that he'd laugh; that it would release the tension and make the whole experience more palatable, while the angel on my other shoulder informed me that it would make him feel like he had been tricked into massaging a predatory homosexual with a thing for fat doctors with clown hands. The angel and devil argued for a little while and the debate was only really put to bed by a squeeze that was just a little too tight and led to me yelping like a dog that had learned to say 'fuck me!' I apologized for shouting 'fuck me'. After all, testicle crush or not, it's not really behaviour befitting a medical examination. To be fair to him, Dr Spadehands offered his own apology in return for over-vigorous kneading. I tried again for small talk and observed that he had a nice tie. He awkwardly replied 'Thanks'. As far as diversionary small talk goes it wasn't going to win any awards (unless there are awards for awkward apparent come-ons

— and I'm not sure who would be giving those out).

As he rummaged around with admirable dexterity for a man with spades instead of hands (save for the dog yelp incident) he decided to take the small talk agenda into his control following my manifest failure. He spotted my Sussex County Cricket Club jumper and used our shared interest in cricket to divert us from the whole ball-touching thing. And while it felt bizarre to be talking cricket with a man as he felt my balls, it probably felt marginally less bizarre than not talking about cricket with a man as he felt my balls. And margins count when your balls are in another man's hands. He told me that in his day (he was in his late fifties) he had been a handy leg spinner. This gave me confidence that my nuts were in the hands of a man with a proven track record in adroitly fingering balls. The topic moved quickly to Kevin Pietersen, England's talismanic but recalcitrant batsman, and he became quite animated about Pietersen's role in the recent dismissal of the England coach. This was something he was clearly annoyed about. So much so that it seemed he had briefly forgotten why we were both there. I was aware that the examination had momentarily ceased as we shared our disgust at

70

Pietersen's attitude. The problem was that I had to figure out how to tell a man who had stopped kneading my balls to start up again. It wasn't a request I was used to so I just looked down and sure enough the search for the lump continued. 'Ah there she is,' he said as he located the cause of my anxiety. I noted the 'she'. Perhaps, like cars and boats, testicular lumps are conferred a female identity?

'Is it a big one?' I asked, and then found myself correcting the initial comment with ' . . . the lump, that is,' before silently cursing myself for it. He said that it wasn't too big; he suspected that it was only a cyst and that it was probably fine. Either way, he would organize for me to have an ultrasound just to check it out properly. We finished the consultation by agreeing categorically that Pietersen had to go as captain.

I then beat as hasty a retreat as possible to an outside world where I wouldn't be having my balls felt by an uncomfortable stranger.

Length of wait
It was an early appointment so only about five minutes this time. This I found immensely disappointing and dispiriting. Since I was about to walk into a room where a complete stranger, with hands that could be

71

used for crushing cows, would fondle my balls, I was hoping that the wait would be at least an hour. I wanted there to be four old people in front of me who took five minutes just to walk to the doctor's office before spending an hour in there talking about the warts on their cat's arse before discovering that the nice man wasn't a vet. Five minutes was an almighty let-down.

Gregory House index (diagnostic capacity)
This probably wasn't a case that would have stretched many doctors. Find a lump and then refer it to another doctor who has a lump machine that can tell whether that lump is nasty or not. It's not up there with fibromyalgia or lupus (numbers two and three in the top ten difficult diseases to diagnose, apparently). That said, credit where it is due. After inspection he told me he suspected it was a benign cyst and that I had nothing to worry about — and he was absolutely right.

Successful outcome?
Put simply, yes.

Sympathetic and professional health care?
I've had my fair share of difficult appointments, and doctors always seem to handle

them well. This appointment was no exception. Yes, there was a momentarily firm squeeze which brought tears to my eyes, but on the whole he was gentle and reassuring and he visibly worked to make a difficult occasion more palatable, especially bearing in mind my own ham-fisted attempts to reduce any discomfort. However, I suppose there was one thing I could mention. Bearing in mind the well-known fact that men are often too embarrassed to go to their doctors for these kinds of intimate inspections, I was kind of hoping for a little bit of praise for turning up in the first place. You know, a kind of pat on the back for being brave, maybe even a lollipop. However, on reflection this is less indicative of an unsympathetic health service and more of a man whose arrested development renders him disappointed if his tummy isn't tickled for achieving the most basic goals in life.

Any signs of inefficiency and poor standards?
If there were, I couldn't see them. A five-minute wait for an appointment that I made at a time of my convenience, followed by an accurate ten-minute consultation. A three-week wait for an ultrasound (which I could rearrange for a more appropriate date if it clashed with work), which confirmed that

73

there was nothing to worry about on the day.

Front page heading you won't find in the *Daily Mail*
'Local GP correctly diagnoses benign cyst.'

Foreskins and strokes: how not waiting very long can still be too long

Too often I have heard people engage in prolonged and usually profoundly dull complaints about having to wait forever to see a GP; that you're more likely to get ill waiting in a GP's surgery than if you stay out of it. But my experience is the opposite — I have rarely waited very long (I'd say on average fifteen minutes). I don't ever remember having a bad experience while waiting in a general practice waiting room (well, apart from once, but I'll come to that in a minute).

Waiting to see a GP has always been a less boring event for me than other waits. There is nothing remotely interesting about waiting for a bus or a train or for a takeaway. But a general practice waiting room? It is literally a social compendium of games just waiting to be unlocked. My favourites in no particular order are as follows:

1. **Guess the reason that a patient is there**. This one is only interesting if, after making your diagnosis, you then strike up small talk with the person with the specific intention of finding out why they are there. It's very easy to look like a crank so it's best to play it with older people since they seem more receptive to approaches from chatty oddballs passing the time. Not an easy game; my hit rate has been about 20% over the years.

2. **Spot the hypochondriac.** I read somewhere that one in seven people admits to considering themselves a hypochondriac. Therefore, if there are seven people in the waiting room, the chances are that one of them is full of shit. Forgetting my fragile grip of probability theory for a second, my personal tactic is to watch carefully for the ones who visibly look a little more sorry for themselves when they notice that a stranger (me) is watching them. The player needs to be careful not to confuse patient self-pity with anxiety that a stranger is staring at them. Unlike the previous game, there is no cast-iron way to confirm diagnosis so it would be a difficult game to sell on *Dragon's Den*.

3. **Spot the terminals**. This game resides at the more macabre end of the surgery

parlour games spectrum and involves figuring out whose symptoms (e.g. limp, cough, frailness) can be most easily attributed to a fatal illness. Stage two involves figuring out how much time they have left. The game gets particularly interesting if you then share this prognosis with the patient.

4. **Who could I beat in an arm wrestle?** This is especially gratifying if you are surrounded by sickly pensioners.

5. **Who is the tallest?** OK, so not all of the games are especially inventive, but you'd be surprised how much fun you can have guessing the height of people who are sitting down. (Or maybe you wouldn't.)

Now for that one negative experience. It happened in my local GP's waiting room when a rather intense-looking man in his fifties sat down next to me. I picked up a magazine on the table. It was one of those boring health brochures that show how happy people are if they eat salad and don't smoke. As I leafed through it I came to a page that contained two articles: one appeared to be on foreskin hygiene and the other on strokes.

I wasn't really looking at either, just flicking, when the man next to me, obviously spotting the foreskin article, said quite loudly,

'I can't understand why you'd have it snipped off.' I froze momentarily as I tried to figure out if a complete stranger had really just tried to instigate a foreskin conversation with me in a busy waiting room. I figured that this probably couldn't have happened and that he was talking to someone else. So I ignored it. Told myself to just keep staring at the magazine and this potentially unwanted social catastrophe would disappear.

But it didn't disappear. It couldn't have disappeared less if it had put on a bright pink t-shirt and danced around in front of me. Instead, my new friend confided to me very loudly that he was glad he wasn't Jewish because he didn't know what he'd do without his foreskin. OK, now it was official. If it wasn't before, it was now a code-red situation — a stranger was trying to have a loud conversation with me about foreskins in a public place. To be specific, in an otherwise completely silent room with about twenty people all showing visible relief that they had not been picked for the public foreskin conversation. I really was taking one for the proverbial team here.

'Unless it was for health reasons; then it would be OK,' he reasoned, suddenly content that he had found a way to lose his foreskin that he would be comfortable with. He was looking at me for a response (as were the twenty other people eager to hear my views on foreskin hygiene). 'Yes, then it would be OK,' I said, while trying not to make eye contact. Everything about my tone of voice screamed, 'Please make that be the end of the conversation. I beg of you, please.'

A brief pause ensued. I allowed myself to dream that maybe that was it. Maybe I had navigated these particular embarrassing social waters and had reached calmer climes.

'Or if it was too long. You know? If your hood was too long.' Oh no, he's just getting started here.

OK, it was clear that I was going to need to mobilize my very best 'don't talk to me' tactics. The question was: which of my 'get a strange man to stop talking about foreskins' techniques was going to work best here? First I tried the obvious one. I opted for complete radio silence. The odd nod but strictly no words. This is usually a pretty strong tactic. However, against Mr Foreskin it wasn't even touching the sides. He was still talking. It was becoming obvious that an articulated lorry full of people visibly not listening to him was not going to stop this guy. He continued to debate, mainly with himself, whether the foreskin was in fact a vestigial feature of the body, that is, whether it had any real use. 'I mean, I don't suppose I've ever really needed mine, you know, and apparently they get dirty, sometimes very dirty.' I think he then asked me about the evolutionary significance of the foreskin. He had obviously mistaken me for someone with a better than average working knowledge of male genitals. I mumbled, 'They're like appendixes and tonsils, I suppose.' I was hoping that articulating specific vestigial structures might get him to talk about appendicitis or something. I was wrong.

'Yeah, but they're not wrapped around your cock.' It was a very powerful medical observation and was delivered with the tone of a man who had out-thought his conversational companion.

'No, no, I suppose not,' I conceded.

I don't have much to say about foreskins at the best of times. So I moved on to the next strategy. I changed the subject. I looked back at my magazine and tried to steer him on to the stroke article. All of a sudden strokes, as a conversation piece, had never been so attractive. I pointed out that this was a nasty thing to suffer, especially when your mouth goes all funny (suddenly mindful that I hadn't checked whether anyone in the waiting room looked like they had had a stroke). He wasn't playing ball. He acknowledged my

79

deviation and shared a few reflections on strokes (they are a bastard apparently) but once the conversation went dry again he looked wistfully into the distance and said 'Strokes and foreskins, eh? Strokes and foreskins — we're all just animals at the end of the day, aren't we?'

I literally didn't know what to say in response to this, so I moved to strategy three. I pretended to be in pain. This one is only to be used in social emergencies. I took my breath in sharply and held my side. 'Are you OK?' he enquired.

Bingo! I thought. At last, we have him off foreskins. 'Yeah, fine, I'm just . . . ' I started, before I was interrupted by him making a joke along the lines of 'It's not your foreskin, is it?' after which he laughed like a drain for what seemed like a full calendar year. A few other patients also laughed, but they were laughing at me trying to manage my new foreskin-obsessed friend. 'No,' I sighed. 'It's not my foreskin.' And with that I ceased my futile attempt to divert his attention by pretending to be in pain.

A few new people came into the waiting room during the course of the conversation. Now, unlike those already present, these people didn't know that I was being forced into a foreskin conversation with an oddball who'd clearly given his carer the slip. I don't know why it was important, but I wanted to send out some kind of signal to say to the new arrivals that we were not just a couple of mates shooting the breeze about dick sheaths. For those of you out there who haven't had the pleasure of trying to signal to a complete stranger using only your eyes that the loud conversation you are having about foreskins was not your idea, it is really quite a difficult thing to do. You can do humour with your eyes; you can do worry, anger, surprise and a whole host of emotions. But 'this foreskin conversation isn't my fault' isn't so easy. As I blinked desperately at the newcomers, I suddenly realized that it had gone quiet on the foreskin conversation front. Perhaps he'd finally decided to move on.

'Only I used to know a lot about foreskins.'

Jesus Christ, I was now starting to look for hidden cameras. But while I was dying to knock this conversation on the head I have to admit that this latest statement had piqued my interest. How could someone possibly have known a lot about foreskins in the past but not know about them any longer? Had he once been a foreskin surgeon but, now retired, was no longer *au fait* with the latest advances? Had he once written a book about foreskins that was now wildly out of date?

Perhaps he used to collect foreskins like some people collect coins before some obscure change in the law rendered the continuation of the practice impossible? I knew I was making a serious mistake in asking him, of course. I knew that I shouldn't have encouraged him, but at this stage I simply couldn't help it. I had to ask. 'Oh yeah, how come?'

'I had an infection once so I read up about them. It was full of pus and I had warts on it. It was an absolute warzone down below; you could have put a police cordon around it,' he said, laughing. Just when I thought that there wasn't a subject that I wanted to talk to a stranger about in a public place less than foreskins, he went on to talk about genital warts. It was my own fault, really; an STD was always going to be the reason. I was going to have to pull out the final tactic, only to be used in really extreme circumstances. I pulled out my mobile phone and pretended I had a call I had to take. Obviously for this to work you need to switch it to 'silent,' lest it actually go off when you're pretending that you are already using it. Luckily I didn't have to do this for long because, as excruciating as the wait felt, like most waits in my surgery, it lasted only about fifteen minutes. It just so happened that it felt like fifteen hours.

Length of wait
Fifteen minutes. No more, no less. I've spent more time waiting for buses than I have GPs. Not bad for a system riddled with inefficiency.

Gregory House index (diagnostic capacity)
I did learn something about how to diagnose genital warts.

Successful outcome?
I know a lot more about strangers' foreskins now than I did before going in that day. I consider that a deeply unsuccessful outcome.

Sympathetic and professional health care?
I answered Foreskin Man's incessant questions with what I considered to be an extreme amount of patience, so all in all, yes.

Any signs of inefficiency and poor standards?
Yes. GP waiting rooms should have signs on the walls that tell people not to talk to strangers about their genitals.

Front page heading you won't find in the *Daily Mail*
'All in all, people don't wait very long to see their GPs.'

83

People in trying circumstances

One of the things that we, or at least I, tend to take for granted about the people who work in the NHS is the extent to which they help people during particularly trying times in their lives. Whether it be patients or their family members, they tend to perform often complex and protracted medical procedures that require working sympathetically with people whose minds are pretty scattered. And, in my experience, they do it very well. On this count, I'm reminded of a holiday in Majorca in my early twenties. After one night of binge drinking combined with food poisoning I found myself hallucinating at 3 a.m. in my hotel. My partner said she was going to get a doctor. The problem was that she came back with the pool cleaner. Or at least a man who looked, to a hallucinating mind, an awful lot like the pool cleaner. As he drew out a syringe I asked what the pool cleaner was doing with a syringe. I was told to relax and that this was a doctor. As the pool cleaner/doctor tried once more to stab some fluid into my arm, I asked him in a mix of broken Spanish and English (which I suspect was just English with a cringeworthy Spanish accent) why he had been cleaning the pool earlier. He didn't have an answer for this, which I took as him being exposed for the fraud he was. I was told again by my partner that he was a doctor and that we should trust him but I responded to this by enquiring why, if he was a doctor, was he wearing shorts and why were his ears so big (the temperature had made me delusional and turned his ears into appendages of rabbit proportions). The pool cleaner left, deflated.

Of course, the pool cleaner didn't actually work for the NHS. Perhaps a more pertinent example happened when I was on my way to Charing Cross Hospital for a sleep EEG. EEGs measure brain activity and are apparently particularly useful for assessing epilepsy when the patient is sleeping. I was told to stay up the night before the appointment so that I would fall asleep for the EEG.

Now I thought to myself that this can't be too hard. Having googled 'sleep deprivation' I found that Maureen Weston holds the current world record for sleep deprivation without stimulants, a staggering eighteen days. Apparently, though, a Thai Ngoc, from Vietnam, claimed not to have slept for thirty-three years, saying that it had no effect, as he could still carry a 100 kg bag of pig feed for 4 km. I thought, if they can do that, then I can at least do one night. So I sat up all night watching old reruns of TV series from the 1980s. Through this I learned five things:

1. Hazzard County would benefit from the involvement of a US federal police presence.
2. Programme planners are convinced that deaf people only come out at night.
3. After a while, if you were B.A. Baracus you would probably come to the conclusion that it was best only to drink milk that you had personally sourced. There are only so many times that you can drug a giant sociopath before you begin to think he needs to take a bit of responsibility for his own welfare.
4. No matter what time of day he is shown, Jeremy Kyle is still unbearable.
5. I do not have Thai Ngoc's stamina.

Sure enough, I'd had about thirty hours of non-sleep when I set off to the hospital on the day of the appointment. However, I wasn't carrying 100 kg of pig feed anywhere and I was still absolutely knackered. So much so that I could barely keep my eyes open. I don't know what the Vietnamese is for 'utter lightweight' but I suspect I would find out if I ever met Thai Ngoc. As I was walking to the hospital I actually fell asleep. I've never fallen asleep walking before and it's quite an unusual experience. I realized that things were much more serious than I had originally thought when I saw a dog with two wheels instead of back legs. (I assumed that this was the sleep deprivation talking; that I must be delusional. I've learned since that sometimes when dogs lose the use of their rear legs, owners can replace them with a wheeled contraption that allows them to continue to get about, a little bit like a dog wheelchair. At the time, though, I couldn't have been more unsettled by this little pooch if he had been holding a flick knife and telling me he was going to make me his bitch. I literally ran away from him.) After a while I got to the hospital a little out of breath, but it looked like I'd lost the freaky cyborg dog, so that was good.

After navigating my way to the EEG suite I told the nurse that I was glad that I had made it here because I'd just seen a dog that looked like Robocop. I took this as evidence that I probably needed to sleep. She asked me whether it had been wearing a helmet. I think she was just humouring me so I told her what it looked like. She confirmed with a benign laugh that it wasn't a Robodog but a disabled dog with a tech-savvy owner. I then made some kind of awkward joke about dog Paralympics. In the uncomfortable gap that followed, I started to think a little bit harder on the whole Robocop dog thing.

'I suppose, on reflection, if you were going to try to build a Robocop dog, you would probably do more than just give it a couple of stainless steel back wheels. You'd need to give it a visor and helmet and a gun and protective armour. And it's a big financial outlay to make on a creature which is probably just going to go and take a shit in the corner. I mean, you can put whatever you want on it; it's not necessarily going to go and catch criminals, is it?'

'I hadn't really given it any thought, love.'

'No, me neither until now,' I back-pedalled.

My fatigue was beginning to reveal itself in the most brutal fashion. I was normally able to keep these kinds of thoughts to myself but sleep deprivation had made my defences weak and allowed some of my inane thoughts to seep out. Anyway, the nurse obviously realized she needed to take the reins if we were going to move the conversation on from dogs in wheelchairs. She asked whether I'd managed to stay awake all night and I confirmed that I had for thirty hours, but that I had seemed to lapse into micro-sleeps while walking here. I told her that I assumed this was normal for someone who has been sleep-deprived as long as I had, but her response, while courteous and kind, suggested that it wasn't really and that I was probably just a bit weak. Feeling a little stung by this, I decided to put her on the spot. She saw people who were sleep-deprived all the time so I asked her how I looked. I asked her to grade me out of ten where ten is looking fine and one is looking like Keith Richards. Either through boredom or a desire not to disappoint me she noted that no two faces were alike so it was hard to tell.

'What about identical twins?' I babbled, and to her credit she didn't even roll her eyes.

'Maybe a three?' she said, obviously realizing that it was going to be the quickest way of shutting me up. 'Or perhaps a four,' she corrected herself, after noticing my disappointment. And then it was time to do the sleep.

The problem was that I couldn't sleep. I had a choice at this point. I could just wait patiently and allow myself to fall asleep eventually or I could bitch and bleat about it like a spoilt child. I chose the latter and proceeded to moan at her incessantly about the paradox of being too tired to sleep. I suspect that I was making her quite sleepy. I also pointed this paradox out.

And so it went on with periods of silence punctuated by my observing that I wasn't sleeping yet. I pointed out that the wires on my head were making it difficult. She responded by asking, I think with a hint of sarcasm, whether I'd like her to take them off.

I then told her that I was going to try to count sheep. There was no answer to this. I got to about fifty and told her that this wasn't working either. Still no answer. I thought at this point I might literally have bored her to death. I didn't want to open my eyes in case I saw a portly nurse swinging from a beam. I kept my eyes closed but shared with her that counting sheep wasn't really a very effective method, that counting Noel Edmonds would be better for me because I find him particularly boring.

'If you try to settle down you'll probably find it easier getting to sleep.'

A further long gap while I tried to get to sleep.

'Do you know there's a bloke in Vietnam who claims not to have slept for thirty-three years. He carries 100 kg bags of pig feed for 4 km every day. Sounds like a bullshitter to me. I mean, seriously, you can see him sitting there in the pub in Vietnam telling all his mates that he can hold his breath longer than a fish or something.'

Silence.

'I knew a lad at school who was a bullshitter. He said he'd beaten Ross Kemp in an arm wrestle and that Ross Kemp had nicknamed him 'champ'. Or was it 'superstar', I can't remember now . . . '

This was the final straw. My sleep-addled ramblings had gone too far. She went off. I thought she was going to come back with a mallet but when she came back it wasn't a mallet she had but something else. 'Would you wear this mask?' Now I'm no Brad Pitt but this seemed quite extreme. Maybe she had become sick of having to look at my face while I didn't fall asleep. I was given a sleep mask, following which I observed that it was really dark. And then promptly fell asleep.

Length of wait
Between the initial consultation and sleep EEG it was about two months. Between arriving for the EEG and falling asleep it was about the same time.

Gregory House index (diagnostic capacity)
Nothing to diagnose here.

Successful outcome?
Very. It was a slow start but I got the sleep

EEG out of the way and I was on my way home an hour after I fell asleep. Can't complain.

Sympathetic and professional health care?
The very definition of it. I think my sleep-deprived ramblings could have got most vicars to strangle me.

Any signs of inefficiency and poor standards?
Not in the slightest. I was straight in; treated with an underserving amount of patience and compassion; and then whisked out. I was even given a free lesson in canine wheelchair culture.

Front page heading you won't find in the *Daily Mail*
'Nurse remains calm and professional amid mindless drivel.'

The Hampstead ball-wrecker

Up until now this book has largely been full of tales that glorify the NHS. Whether this is due to the efficiency of the services they offer, the attitudes of the staff or the standards they hold to, it has been a tale of one man's admiration for this group of people who put him together again when things looked like they might be falling apart. There have been a number of stories here about how the British National Health Service is a modern wonder of the world and how the people who run it are somewhere between angels and saints.

Thus far you've probably come to the conclusion that I am a fairly partisan observer of the NHS. Well, here I'm going to sully the waters for the first time.

In this section I'm going to focus on the inarguable fact that the NHS is a hazard for men who are 5 ft 8 in tall. If you are a woman who is 5 ft 8 in tall, you have little to worry about. If you are a man 5 ft 7 in and below, or 5 ft 9 in and above, then the NHS poses you no threat. But 5 ft 8 in? You're in trouble. Here we *do* have a failing NHS where private health care may have a genuine and meaningful role to play in the nation's health.

I came by this revelation when I used to work at The Royal Free Hospital in North London. I wasn't a medic; rather, I was an academic researcher working in the department of psychiatry. There are two interesting things about this department. The first is that in three years there I never saw a single patient. Toward the end I came to think that I was the only patient they had and my particular delusion was that I was a researcher on an EU-funded, primary-care, mental-health project. An elaborate delusion, but not an impossible one. The second interesting thing was that unless you were a psychiatrist, you didn't get a window for your office. This was fine but it meant that you needed to get out and walk around every once in a while. Now, as this was a hospital, there was a bit of a shortage of exciting places to go for a five-minute break.

My go-to place for excitement was the hospital shop on the ground floor. Firstly, because it sold cheddar and onion McCoys (my favourite crisp) and, secondly, because it sold cheddar and onion McCoys. Every now and again, when I felt the walls closing in a bit, I would hop down to the shops to indulge myself. The zone by the lift on the ground floor was a pretty high-traffic area with people being quickly wheeled around in moveable beds. What happened in this maelstrom of traffic was that I was hit not once, not twice, but three times — right in the balls by these hospital beds. It was here that I came to the realization that if you worked in a hospital and you were around 5 ft 8 in, then walking around was a little bit like a cheap and fairly tedious version of *The*

Hunger Games — except that rather than teenagers getting killed, short men get smacked in the nuts. On two of these occasions I was hit so hard that I was completely floored, lying on the ground, cradling my balls and mumbling whispered expletives.

Now I admit that I was partly culpable for some of these hits. Once I get cheddar and onion McCoys in my head I tend to lose focus. What descends on my mind might usefully be described as a 'crisp mist'. The first time it happened the injury was compounded by both the orderly and a very old patient in the bed laughing about having clocked me in the balls. The patient looked pretty ill with an oxygen mask and a gazillion tubes coming out of him, but he took the time to take his mask off so that he could laugh at me properly.

Now this is an odd situation because your natural response can't really be expressed. Essentially, you have been hit by a very ill man and another man who is helping a very ill man. Despite being angry and in pain you can't really say anything. There are certain rules that most of us in society manage to follow: don't make pregnant women cry, don't kick puppies, don't call a terminally ill man a dickhead — that sort of thing. The patient said, 'Christ! His balls will be worse than mine' — a comment that set both him and his orderly laughing again following a brief sojourn of sympathy when they asked me how I was. The old man snickered that I needed the bed more than him so that I could be taken to the 'ball ward', before mumbling something about national service sorting me out and being driven off by the orderly. I could hear their chuckles echoing down the corridor. Let's call that 'ball trauma one'.

A few weeks later I encountered ball trauma number two. This time the bed was moving with such force and velocity that when it hit me I actually folded over onto the bed with my head more or less in the lap of a middle-aged woman in a hospital gown that was a good two sizes too small for her (on a good day). The up-side of this particular trauma was that even though it struck me in the balls, it didn't hurt so much as wind me since the bar at the end of the bed slammed right into my midriff. Don't get me wrong — my balls were sore. But in the list of priorities at that point, struggling to breathe came first.

Being British, I engaged in the time-honoured practice of apologizing for things that weren't my fault whilst trying to get my breath back. The woman then turned to her orderly and asked with no little disdain, 'Honestly, what was he *thinking?*' Her tone of voice implied that my face landing in her lap had not been the result of an unfortunate and unforeseen high-speed collision between a woman on her way to a consultation and a greedy bastard running to get his hands on his favourite crisps. Rather, it suggested that this had somehow been a logical part of my plan to have my balls crushed.

As they trundled off, I sat down for a bit on a nearby seat and realized that I was going to have to change my approach to walking around the hospital from here on in. No more the carefree wanderer of times gone by. The hospital was a veritable maze of fast-moving beds, and they were all set with seemingly malevolent precision at the same ball-terrorizing default height. I gave the matter some serious thought. The only solutions I could come up with were either to wear a cricket box permanently, walk backwards everywhere or borrow my wife's high heels. A quick summary of the respective merits of these options revealed that none was perfect.

Cricket box
PROS: offers lasting protection no matter the velocity of the bed.
CONS: If I did get struck on the cricket box

there would be a loud plasticky noise.

Walking backwards
PROS: my arse provides a lot of protection.
CONS: reduced vision may make collisions more likely. Might also get sectioned too.

Wearing high heels
PROS: would look taller than I actually am.
CONS: Would look extremely strange. Blisters a certainty and a twisted ankle or two also a realistic possibility.

Back to the drawing board.

Now the time has come for me to tell you of ball trauma number three. By this point life was beginning to feel like a particularly unimaginative remake of *Groundhog Day*. This latest trauma was right in the sore spot and I instinctively fell to one knee and shouted 'Oh come on, enough of this already. What's wrong with you fucking people?' Understandably, this confused my new orderly/patient combination since they were unaware of my previous history of testicle interceptions. This one was painful. Oh, good God, was it painful! I found myself frozen on one knee in front of this trolley, looking for all the world like a man who had decided to propose marriage to his ill partner in hospital and was fumbling in his trouser pockets for the ring. I hung in the marriage proposal position for a while, partially owing to the pain and partly as a passive-aggressive punishment for my new attackers since they were blocked as long as I was there.

Clearly confused, the orderly said, 'What do you mean by 'you people'?' I looked up and, on noticing that he was black, was suddenly seized by a wave of middle-class liberal panic.

'Orderlies in this hospital,' I blurted out. 'I wasn't talking about — you know . . . black people. I'm not a racist.'

'OK, mate, easy. I'm sure you're not.'

'It's just that you people keeping ramming my balls — porters, that is; not black . . . not . . . you know.'

'Maybe you need to be a little more careful; watch where you're going?' The patient on the trolley was unconscious and looked in a really bad way so I felt a bit bad about blocking their way while cradling my throbbing balls. 'Sorry, I need to get going now,' the porter said politely. I cleared his path, slumped against the wall and nodded goodbye.

Length of wait
Not long enough. My balls were getting

crushed with clockwork regularity.

Gregory House index (diagnostic capacity)
Since the only person that linked all three incidents was me, I begrudgingly came to the conclusion that I needed to take responsibility for the safety of my own testicles.

Successful outcome?
No. My balls *really* hurt three times.

Sympathetic and professional health care?
The professionalism that the orderlies showed in making sure that my nuts got crushed was laudable.

Any signs of inefficiency and poor standards?
Yes, the NHS clearly doesn't give a shit about the balls of 5 ft 8 in men who aren't looking where they're going because they are focusing on stuffing their faces with crisps. Bring in the private sector!

Front page heading you won't find in the *Daily Mail*
'NHS has it in for men who are 5 ft 8 in. Or at least for their balls.'

Astounding quality of care, even for a grownup who fell off a scooter

I used to live with some friends in Croydon, on top of a steep hill. As opening lines to paragraphs go I realize that this isn't the most promising. However, the steep hill bit is relevant. One day a friend of one of my flatmates decided to pop over on his scooter. I seem to remember this being quite a novel item at the time and, after trying assiduously to work out what an adult man, who wasn't on his way to donate toys to a children's charity, was doing with a scooter, I watched as everyone had a bash on it. Even though I was quite aware that scooters, along with skateboards and Simply Red CDs, were on the long list of things that all right-thinking adults shouldn't touch with a barge pole, I decided that I would have a little try too. I mean, what could possibly go wrong? After all, you're only an inch off the ground.

However, rather than scoot along the flat path outside our house, I decided — despite never having been on one of these contraptions — to scoot down the steep hill. I can't really be sure but I think I might have been trying to show off, as ludicrous as a 26-year-old trying to impress other 26-year-olds with speedy scooter-skills might sound. I suspect that the scooter might have woken the barely concealed show-off child inside me. The last time I remember doing something like this was in 1984 when I tried to jump over a line of six nervous children from my estate using only a flimsy ramp and a Raleigh Commando. That ended in what might optimistically be called 'qualified success' as I landed on the heads of the last two children on the line. So, the signs that this was going to be a disaster were there from the start.

So off I scooted down the hill and it wasn't long before I was surprised by two key things. The first was how quickly these little things could shift. The second related to the fact that I had mounted the scooter standing with one foot square on top of the other. This turned out to be more important than I had anticipated when it came to trying to locate the brake. As I picked up pace, I suddenly remembered that there was a very busy main road at the bottom of this hill. With my brake foot trapped and an already fearsome pace picked up, I was beginning to visualize the headline in the *Croydon Gazette*: 'Dickhead Dies On Scooter'. OK, that might not have been the exact wording they'd have used, but you get the gist.

As the road fast approached I realized I

had three options. The first was to just plough on ahead, hoping there were no cars. This was immediately ranked a distant third. The second was to turn the steering bar and steer into the wall at the side of the pavement. The third was to try to jump off and quickly get up to speed by running.

Naturally, as always in moments of potential danger, my first thought was, 'What would the Fall Guy do in this situation?' Colt Seavers never lets me down, and nor did he in this crisis. He spoke to me and told me that I was going to have to jump off and quickly get my feet up to speed. Of course, I was jumping off a vehicle that was moving about 20 mph with feet that were prepared to move at about 5 mph. This disparity meant that as my feet hit the ground I looked like the only gerbil at gerbil school too simple to figure out how to move its feet on its exercise wheel. The one that all the other gerbils laugh at. Actually, that's not fair: even a simple gerbil would have been as confused by my lack of foot speed as my onlooking friends were.

I hit the ground with some force and some pain, and as I lay at the bottom of the hill surveying my cuts and bruises, I reflected that maybe comparing myself to the Fall Guy might have been a little premature. Luckily there was an old lady at the bus stop next to my prone form and she helpfully pointed out that I had been going too fast. Looking back now I don't know what I would have done without that observation. Sometimes God really does send his angels. I think she then called me a dickhead. And she gave me a smile that said, 'Yes, that's right, I did call you a dickhead but I'm so old that you can't possibly try to call me on it.'

Anyway, that was that. Or at least I thought it was until I woke up the next day and noticed that my hand had ballooned up like Violet Beauregarde. It was clear that I was going to have to go to Accident and Emergency.

When I got there it was mercifully empty, with only a few stragglers occupying the waiting room chairs. The two-hour wait would have been quite manageable had I not had to endure a prolonged argument between one couple about whether the man fancied Kirstie Allsop from *Location, Location, Location* more than he did his partner. Had he been on the ball there were a number of ways that he could probably have killed this conversation stone-dead. However, acknowledging that Kirstie had a great rack sent him very much down the wrong road for that. His partner was furious, and snapped that, after she went to bed, he probably tugged himself off while watching *Location, Location, Location*. Now at this point a simple denial would have been in order but instead his defence was that *Location, Location, Location* was on too early for that. He then tried to salvage things by pointing out that he didn't even like brunettes, to which she replied, quick as a flash: 'Yeah, but you do like big tits!' Now he was back under the cosh and really needed to up his game. Instead he replied, 'Well, yeah.' Checkmate, or so it seemed until, after a period of intense thought, he mumbled, 'I like small ones, too'. To be fair, this was turning out to be quite an amusing exchange; certainly better than the television in the corner, on which some poor sap was being grilled by Jeremy Kyle.

Anyway, eventually they both went off in a huff, which meant I was stuck with Jeremy Kyle. The scenario was quite routine. An angry-looking lady (with a minimal amount of teeth) was accusing a befuddled-looking man (with even fewer teeth) of being the father of her unborn child. He was firmly denying this. It to'd and fro'd and by the end, I won't lie, I wanted to know myself. (I was backing the mum.) The problem was that the nurse came out at just the point where I was going to get the big reveal. I momentarily considered asking whether he would mind waiting until I found out whether Eugene was the dad, or maybe whether I could move back a place in the queue, but I thought better of it. After all, it's called Accident and Emergency for a reason.

So I ambled through to the treatment room and faced the standard questions. Unfortunately, I had been too busy with accidents of birth and toothless simpletons to really prepare for the 'So how did you do this?' question in the waiting room. Shit. I needed to think quickly so as to try not to look like a complete idiot. I thought hard but sadly the best I could come up with was, 'It was a just a thing really.'

'A thing?' the doctor replied.

Seemingly we weren't going to move on from this as quickly as I'd hoped. I suppose to be fair nobody was ever going to reply, 'Oh, it was a *thing*, was it? Well, that's cleared up now.' Keen for my evasiveness not to be interpreted as covering up for domestic violence I decided to reply, 'Yes, a scooter.' Of course, she looked at me as if I'd announced with pride that my middle name was 'Buttplug'. I suppose I figured that I could still wrestle some kind of dignity from this exchange because I added ' . . . but it was an adult one'.

She then said, as she looked over my

swollen hand, that she thought that they only stood an inch off the ground. I replied, with an authority not befitting my predicament, that you can still get your foot trapped one inch off the ground. 'After all, you can drown a man with a teaspoon of water,' I added helpfully.

'Is that so?' she replied drily, before taking me carefully through the X-ray slides (I'd chipped a bone in my hand) via the light box on the wall. We went through the different bones in the hand, what had happened to my bone and what the likely prognosis would be, and this in a very busy casualty department where time was clearly at a premium. I remember leaving thinking that this level of care and attention was a little bit special. So much so that I even wrote a letter to the manager of the hospital's A&E, probably the only time that I have ever done so (and received a letter of thanks to boot for taking the time to give them feedback on the excellent care and attitude of their staff). I was struck by the way the doctor did not rush me through, 'process me' or move me on. Instead, she took the time to explain things to me with patience and care. It was simply superb, and my good care was just one of the many, many examples of this that happen all over the country on a daily basis.

The problem is that we won't see this kind of event when we pick up the papers and read about what is happening in our NHS. A story entitled 'Fat bloke who is not very important is treated like he is really important in a provincial A&E' isn't really going to shift copies. So instead the papers that delight in bashing the NHS will wait patiently, wading through their backlog of stories on benefit scroungers, red tape, and the EU for the one in a million story of a bloke having his kidney taken out by mistake. Now, of course, this is a bad thing; all serious medical mistakes are bad things. But they don't happen very often. This is why, unlike good-quality care, they count as being news. Unfortunately, this means that a sizeable portion of the public get the idea that a man having breasts sewn onto him by mistake (I think I read about that somewhere but it might have been a dream) is commonplace in our hospitals.

Length of wait
Two hours in casualty.

Gregory House index (diagnostic capacity)
I had chipped a bone in my hand and their X-ray found it. Can't ask for any more really. Well, maybe apart from a Kirstie Allsop tits

debate, which I also got, free of charge.

Successful outcome?
As successful as they come. A hand/wrist support for four weeks and then I was all fixed.

Sympathetic and professional health care?
As good as I've ever had.

Any signs of inefficiency and poor standards?
Yes. Someone really needs to design a scooter with a handbrake. Either that or some kind of scanning device that can identify and reject cretins.

Front page heading you won't find in the *Daily Mail*
As above.

The health visitor

Health visitors are UK community health nurses who have undertaken further training to work as part of primary health care teams. Limited resources and staff within the NHS have traditionally meant that their work has been focused on childhood development and they usually work with mothers once postpartum care is handed over from midwives. Now it seems to me that, of all the medical professionals doing their work around the country right now, the health visitor is the one with the lowest esteem in the public eye. If you were an alien on a day trip from Mars you could be forgiven for thinking that their official title was *'bloody health visitors'* on account of the number of times you would probably hear that word prefix their official title.

The primary problem that faces health visitors is that it is their job to advise, counsel and address difficulties that don't have a neat, one-size-fits-all solution. They don't get to treat things like diabetes and strokes, where you do a test to isolate the extent of the problem, and provide some form of medicine to deal with it. Oh, no. Health visitors get these kinds of problems to deal with:

- My breasts hurt when he feeds.
- He won't stop crying when he gets put down.
- He won't sleep more than one hour.
- He won't open his eyes.
- He won't close his eyes.

Now health visitors can and do make

suggestions for possible approaches that might help these things but, essentially, the practice of advising on feeding, care, and support to both babies and parents is a fatally flawed one. The reason for this is relatively simple and is best highlighted by trying to address the issue of a baby that refuses to sleep through the night (or more than two hours for that matter). You see, regardless of what you try, and regardless of the intervention suggested, the baby's response is always 'fuck you'. How about feeding more for longer? Baby's response: 'fuck you'. How about getting into an early night-time routine? Baby's response: 'fuck you'. How about a blackout blind if it's too light? Baby's response? You've guessed it: 'fuck you'.

Now, of course, babies can't actually say 'fuck you' yet, and perhaps the reason that children don't learn to speak until eighteen months onward is not because it takes time for their vocal apparatus to develop, but because it is evolution's way of protecting parents from being told 'fuck you' 250 times a day. Instead, babies cry incessantly and loudly. (But make no mistake — they are saying 'fuck you'.)

Essentially, the problems that new parents are faced with are intractable for the length of time that it takes for their baby to get bored

111

with saying 'fuck you'. But even in this context, health visitors can be incredibly useful; a fact often missed because they don't bring with them instant solutions to the problems at hand. Our daughter didn't prepare us much for our son. She, as far as babies go, was relatively disinclined to tell us to go fuck ourselves. She ate well, slept pretty well after the first month or so and was a relatively content little thing. But our boy was quite different. He spent the first year telling us to go fuck ourselves three times a night. Every single night. You would have thought that he would have wanted a night off once in a while, maybe do something different, catch a show, see the sights, but nope. He just wanted to cry and be awake. So we asked the health visitor for advice.

Up until that point we had received (frequently unasked for) advice from a range of people in our social circle. This led to the uncomfortable realization that the people around me think that I am a moron. Among the various, frankly silly, pieces of advice that I have received on a baby that doesn't sleep are the following:

Make sure he's getting enough food
Shit! Food! Of course, how could we have forgotten? What a shrewd idea. Feed a baby.

How, after months of sleepless nights, could it not have dawned on me to feed him more?

Put him in with his sister
Ah, nice idea. Let's take the child who doesn't sleep, who is saying 'fuck you' three times a night with metronomic regularity, and allow him to ruin the sleep of the only person in the household who is currently getting any. Nobel prizes all around.

Shout back at him
While I could immediately see the value in this approach from my own perspective, it didn't really strike me as having any great long-term potential. This suggestion was made from a person who didn't have children. This is probably a good thing.

Turn on the vacuum cleaner so you can't hear him
If I have to wake up at 1 a.m., 4 a.m. and 4.45 a.m. to turn on a vacuum cleaner, then in a sense I'm not really addressing the issue at hand.

Tickle him
The person who made this suggestion was, unknown to him, immediately relegated to Tier E of the list of people who I would take

advice from. Tier E is for people whose advice is only welcome on subjects of the most minor importance (whether to watch a specific film or not; whether blue is really my colour, etc.). He was previously in Tier B (suggestions for holiday destinations, career advice, that sort of thing).

You need to try Gina Ford
For those of you not familiar with Gina Ford, a day under her sage advice would go like this:

7.21 a.m. Feed child
7.33 a.m. Have a dump
7.37 a.m. Eat three mouthfuls of apple
7.38 a.m. Stroke child's head once
7.39 a.m. Eat two more mouthfuls of apple
7.40 a.m. Drink water
7.41 a.m. Stand up
7.42 a.m. Smile at child
7.43 a.m. Scratch your balls
7.44 a.m. Sit back down

OK, so I don't even have the patience to take you through the first hour of this. Let's just say taking advice from Gina Ford is a no-no. And I would also perhaps issue a little advice of my own to those people who take it upon themselves to offer tips on child-rearing practices without being asked. Unless you have in mind something so revolutionary, so unusual and so unheard of as to evoke a reaction of monumental surprise, it's usually best to just keep it to yourself.

But our health visitor? Well, we figured that she was a professional, that she might just have the magic key that would allow us to move from sleep-deprived hallucinations to just being really, really tired all the time. So we called her and she came over. As we did the introductions and got teas and coffees I mulled over the thorny issue of chloroform. Now I am worldly enough to know that mention of the word 'chloroform' in conjunction with babies is a little bit of a social no-no, but I didn't really know much about the substance itself and wondered whether they might have a baby-friendly variety. For a moment I reflected on how she would respond to the request; if not for my son, then maybe for me. If there wasn't some baby-friendly chloroform we could pump through the whole house, then perhaps I could put some on a handkerchief and put it over my mouth like in the movies; in a sense that might also solve the problem. I realized that my sleep-deprived fantasies were probably best kept festering within the confines of my exhausted skull. That said, could it really hurt to ask?

I tried to edge towards it in the conversation and so asked whether there was anything natural that we could give our boy to help him sleep? This was her chance. I had opened the door for her to suggest this baby-friendly variety of chloroform that I had decided existed. Sadly she slammed it in my face, saying that, while certain medications for itching and pain relief did have an analgesic effect, it wasn't recommended to administer them other than for their primary use. Spoilsport!

Length of wait
We called her on the Monday and she came round the next day. As we had gone eleven months without a night's sleep we figured one more wouldn't make a difference. In fact, we thought this was a pretty good level of service.

Gregory House index (diagnostic capacity)
After a few questions about his feeding quantities and regimes, she gave us some simple, structured advice that we could implement. It wasn't rocket science but might as well have been to us. Go in and pat your child (while not picking them up) in the cot

for a few seconds every ten minutes or so in order that they know you are about, but that they won't be coming out of the cot. Now this initially makes babies, whose little brains already brim with a ferocious nocturnal desire to tell their parents to fuck themselves, go absolutely haywire. At this point, were anyone capable of deciphering babyspeak what they would hear would sound like a drunken brawler with Tourette's being booted out of a Glasgow pub at closing time. Absolutely savage. But since we can't, it just sounds like a bunch of really angry cries. These eventually dissipate as your baby comes to realize that shouting at the top of their voice simply isn't going to cut it anymore. And so they do the next best thing and go to sleep. Eventually.

Successful outcome?
After eleven months and 6,348 night wakes (I had plenty of time to do the calculations) it was over. Four long, difficult nights on from her visit we had our first full night's sleep. Followed by another one. And then another one. There was the odd regression now and again where the urge to say 'fuck you' to us was obviously still too much for our son, but on the whole this midwife had helped us to finally crack it. The impact this woman had

on our day-to-day lives can reasonably be described as immense. This was a real game-changer, a *life*-changer; it was free, and she turned up the next day. A bit like a slightly lazy superhero.

Sympathetic and professional health care?

She was friendly, sympathetic and encouraging and she gave us the feeling that we were doing really well despite being relentlessly knackered. Her advice was constructive and focused, and she helped put into place a possible plan of action while appreciating the efforts that we had made up until that point. Bearing in mind that most of her job must involve dealing with sleep-deprived zombies with significantly reduced levels of tolerance, she was remarkably cheerful, too.

Any signs of inefficiency and poor standards?

Well, she didn't give me any baby-friendly chloroform, but other than that I can't really complain.

Front page heading you won't find in the *Daily Mail*

'Health visitor is really helpful.'

Ice Road Truckers and maternity wards

I have two hobbies that I'm not especially proud of. The first involves searching the internet with my kids for pictures of fat animals and then laughing at them. I'm a well-educated man — an academic, no less. I should be reading Proust and revelling in the finer nuances of Hobbes' *Leviathan*, not laughing at chubby horses. The second and marginally less embarrassing hobby is watching *Ice Road Truckers*. For the uninitiated, *Ice Road Truckers* is a television programme where a group of Alaskan truck drivers drive long distances in cold conditions. That's it. Literally nothing ever happens on the programme. The drivers drive alone so there aren't even any conversations or confrontations. It's literally a camera watching a bunch of fat blokes watching an empty road. And yet it entertains me profoundly. I find myself glued to the screen as I watch these drivers traverse all manner of road hazards which, despite the high-tension music, clearly don't actually exist.

The reason I mention my base tastes here is because *Ice Road Truckers* acts as my default comparison when I consider how tough a job is. Now ice road trucking is a tough gig. We know this because every two minutes the narrator tells us that it's a tough gig. But also because the job entails spending long periods on your own in freezing cold conditions, driving through huge blankets of white that show absolutely no discerning features. Day after day, after day.

I found myself mobilizing my default 'how tough is this job?' comparison when my wife and I went into hospital for the birth of our daughter. What became obvious to me there was just how much work the maternity nurses do during the process. Yes, they do the nursey things like administer pain relief, monitor the health of mother and baby and organize the whole birth process. But they also spend a huge amount of time doing what is known as 'emotion work'. Now your average ice road trucker might give the idea of emotion work short shrift, but it happens and it can be profoundly tiring. Nurses spend so much time supporting both the mother and father, reassuring them, encouraging them, cajoling them and helping with the management of pain. Just watching it looked exhausting. And it was such an important part of our birth experience.

When we first arrived at the hospital we were wheeled into our little room. Well, OK, *I* wasn't wheeled — that would have been a bit odd — but my wife was. We settled down, with my wife managing her contractions amidst A LOT of screaming from the rooms around us from ladies who were obviously further down the line than my wife was.

The nurses told me that I should take this opportunity to rest because I would need to keep my strength up for later. This phrase was repeated to me several times, enough to get me seriously worried. Just what was going to happen that I would need strength for? Had they found some kind of technology that transferred the birth process to me when it all got a bit too much for my wife? It was an ominous thing to hear for a dyed-in-the-wool coward.

For the obvious reason it can be a little uncomfortable speaking about the difficulties of the birth process as a man. The general feeling is one of awkwardness as you sit passively and watch the love of your life in astonishing agony because of something that you both did. A bit like when you're a kid and your friend is getting a bollocking at the front of the class for reading a note that you passed to him. And as you sit and watch him get torn apart you feel all awkward and guilty. Not awkward and guilty enough to own up but a bit awkward and guilty, nevertheless. If I'm honest I kind of expected that to be reflected in the attitudes of the maternity nurses. I kind of expected a 'keep out of our way while we sort out your mess' type of attitude, but, in fact, they couldn't have been kinder or more supportive. They seemed quite happy to neglect my role in all this pain and blood and agony that was happening in front of them. It's difficult to articulate how you feel as a man during the labour process, but the best I can manage is that you feel like you are watching a particularly brutal and bloody boxing match and you are the girl with the card in the breaks between rounds. In some ways, you are integral to the process, but on the whole you are utterly useless.

For the maternity nurses there is a lot to manage and as I sat and stuffed my face with peanuts and sweets to keep my strength up for this ominous event that was coming later, I watched amazed at how much work they did. They were counsellors, nurses and anaesthetists all rolled into one, darting from room to room for long intense shifts where they managed people through the longest, most physically painful and intense event of their lives. The currency of their daily work was the management of utter agony, but the empathy and patience didn't dip once — even for me, sitting in the corner feeling for all the world like one of those bank robbers who gets the gold and then gets trapped in the vault as the bars come down. Different maternity nurses would come in, but the response was always the same.

Since there wasn't much for me to do, I decided to make myself useful and go and get some glitzy magazines that have pictures of Jordan and Peter Andre on the front that suggest they might be back on. You can't provide pain relief; you can't check vital signs; you can't give birth — but you *can* provide a magazine that has a section called 'What were they thinking?' about women who wore dresses that they really shouldn't have. As the hours of labour started to unfold I was told by various maternity nurses that I was doing really well and really helping my wife. This felt a bit odd since I was basically just looking at pictures of Bjork wearing a dead swan, head and all, and eating peanuts. (I mean, to be fair, I was eating them really well — I don't think I spilled a single one.) I have a lot of experience of just standing around doing nothing but up until that point nobody had ever complimented me for it. So that was nice. And they kept asking how I was bearing up. Of course, there is only one answer to this. When you are sat next to your screaming wife who is writhing in agony the question comes to take on a rhetorical quality. As time wore on and tiredness set in, I found myself constructing a list. This one aimed to establish the single most inappropriate response to a maternity nurse who asked you how you were doing. I came up with the following:

1. Bored, actually. How much longer is this going to go on?
2. I've got a little bit of a headache from all the noise. Have you got anything for that?
3. Drained. It's funny because in a way it's every bit as bad for the partners, you know what I mean?
4. Bit concerned about how long this is taking. I'm off out on the piss tonight and could really do with wrapping this up sooner rather than later. Have you got anything that'll speed it up?
5. I'm fine. It's her who's making all the bloody noise.
6. Bit worried, actually. Trying to figure out what to say to my bit on the side — this is our anniversary, you see.
7. I feel a bit like someone's taking the piss. I saw a programme once where a pig gave birth to loads of piglets and it wasn't moaning for gas and air.
8. (Flicking through channels on the telly) Is

there a porn channel on this?

9. Can you guys hold the fort here for an hour? I saw a lovely young thing in the gift shop downstairs and I want to get her number before she clocks off.

I ran them past my wife in a gap between contractions and she agreed that the pig one probably edged it. And so the hours wore on and the pain for my wife grew. Still they kept reassuring, cajoling, motivating and listening. It was a long labour and what was so impressive was that, as they clocked on and off the shifts, the new nurse tended to be every bit as tender, attentive, vigilant, friendly and warm as the one who preceded her. All of them, and we must have seen six through two nights. It was like *Groundhog Day*. I thought eventually we'll find one who can't be arsed, who is standoffish, harassed-looking or bored, but none arrived. While the best that I could do was eat peanuts and make silly lists, these people specialized in making the unbearable bearable, day after night after day. Even ice road truckers don't do that.

Length of wait
Nearly forty-eight hours, but that was my daughter's fault, really.

Gregory House index (Diagnostic capacity)

With the assistance of my lovely wife, I successfully diagnosed the worst possible thing you could say to a maternity nurse.

Successful outcome?

130,345 peanuts eaten and an amazing daughter born. Two great outcomes.

Sympathetic and professional health care?

The most sympathetic and the most professional I think I have ever witnessed. And it happened with the birth of our second child, too, so, unless lightning strikes twice, this might just be how these people operate on a daily basis. Genuinely inspiring.

Any signs of inefficiency and poor standards?

For sure there were a few little clerical errors — for instance, we were taken into the wrong room a few times — but that can be forgiven in the context of the remarkably high standard of care received.

Front page heading you won't find in the *Daily Mail*

'Fat man eating peanuts can't believe how great maternity nurses are.'

Out of hours

As a new parent it can take a little while to come to realize that even very young babies are pretty resilient. We were in this position when our daughter, who was three weeks old at the time, woke up one Sunday morning with a rash covering her from head to toe. Now I can't tell chickenpox from measles from a heat rash, but she was clearly distressed and felt very hot too. So the first thing I did, as you do, was type '3-week-old with all over body rash' into an internet search engine that pays tax in the UK.

This, of course, didn't help because I kept seeing the word 'meningitis'. My anxiety was heightened. I don't really know much about meningitis other than the fact that it is a very bad thing, right up there with Sting, liquorice and Woody Allen films. The one thing that most sites seemed to ask was 'Do they have a temperature?' So this was the next step. Of course, with a 3-week-old baby you can't just ask them to sit still and not move while you take their temperature. As children get older, the staple tricks of bribery and blackmail can get you through most things, but at three weeks they don't really care about getting chocolate or not getting to watch *Peppa Pig*. Rummaging around in the kitchen I found a thermometer. The problem was that it was an underarm thermometer, which means that you have to find a way of holding them still for long enough to take a reading. You might think this would be easy, but even for a 3-week-old girl you actually need four adults to use this device. One to hold the child, one to hold the thermometer, one to hold the child's head and one to fetch you some heroin to take the edge off. Unfortunately, there were only two of us, and it just wasn't happening. I couldn't get a reading from this thermometer for love nor money, although I did manage to get a kick in the balls for my troubles. Back to square one.

I rummaged back in the medical box and this time found one of those snazzy ear thermometers like the ones that doctors themselves use. Turns out my mum, in an unprecedented act of forward-thinking, had bought us one and shoved it in the box. I read the instructions and it said that you had to put it in the ear, press the button and then wait until you heard a bleep. Wow, this sounded easy. The problem was that this thermometer was playing hardball. I tested it out on my own ear and discovered that I was dead. This wasn't an easy way to find out — it was all a little bit Bruce-Willis-at-the-end-of-*The-Sixth-Sense*. What then followed, as my daughter screamed in the background, was farcical. I placed it in her ear but there was no bleep. I took it out and then it bleeped. I put in back in and then it gave a really long bleep and a reading of four degrees. I'm no doctor but I knew this was bollocks. It then gave an even longer bleep followed by no reading. I was losing patience by this point and told the thermometer in no uncertain terms that I did not know what a long bleep signified. It didn't reply so I called it something I won't repeat here. From this I learned that there's nothing to be gained in self-esteem by being reduced to arguing with a small piece of battery-driven plastic. And anyway it didn't even respond. Nothing at all. And then, after a few seconds, a seemingly disembodied bleep. Now I don't speak Thermometerese but I had a feeling that it had taken in my insult, reflected on it and called me something equally unpleasant back.

Anyway I knew how to fix the situation. I did what anyone who is descended from monkeys would do with a finely calibrated and sophisticated piece of micro-electronic engineering. I banged it twice on the table just in case the fine electronic circuitry was malfunctioning as a result of it missing a bang on a wooden surface. Alas not. I had drawn from my intellectual backburner by banging it hard and swearing at it, and it hadn't worked. That was me done. I was clean out of ideas. My wife then went and found the instructions, read them and took the temperature. I contributed by muttering under my breath about how everything in life had to be so complicated and how people didn't have these problems in the 1940s.

To cut a long story short, my daughter's temperature was higher than the healthy range so we popped her in the car and whipped her round to the weekend out-of-hours clinic that was running at the local hospital. I personally feel uneasy entering a hospital unless I see a couple of rake-thin patients in dressing gowns, tubes sprouting from their noses, having a crafty fag outside. Sure enough, I felt a sense of calm come over me as I spotted the obligatory iron-lung smokers in the doorway. Without any sense of apparent irony they were complaining to each other about how the hospital wasn't giving them the best treatment available. I have no doubt that if the hospital had a mouth (and functioning larynx) at that point it would probably have retaliated by suggesting that stuffing a cigarette into the only hole on their face without a tube in it might also be potentially detrimental to their treatment.

Anyway, we got to the out-of-hours

reception. It was a Sunday morning and I wasn't feeling particularly confident that this was going to be a speedy affair. However, in the waiting room there seemed to be only two more sets of patients — a (very) old man and his wife and a family with two boys, one of whom was flicking his brother's ear.

As we took our seats the very old man gave out a sequence of low guttural gasps that suggested he might already have died and was ejecting the last remaining air from his lungs. It got me thinking about what to do if he did die. On the plus side, it would move us up one space in the queue, but on the negative side there would be an old dead man sitting next to me and that can really ruin a Sunday morning. I don't speak from experience here. I've never encountered an old dead man before (can you still be considered old if you're dead?), but our car did once run over a dog on a Sunday trip and that was a real downer. So, on the balance of things I found myself rooting for him to make it, at least as long as we were in the hospital. His wife was reading a yachting magazine, one suspects by way of planning ahead what to do with the life insurance. This seemed a little insensitive to me, especially while he was there.

While we waited, the parents of the two boys entered into a hotly contested debate about the relative merits of getting a dog. He said that they needed a dog and that the boys would love it. She countered that she didn't like dogs and that they were stupid. He said some of them were very bright — after all, you only had to look at guide dogs — to which she responded with the masterstroke that nobody in their family was blind. She suggested a gerbil or a guinea pig, to which he moaned that you couldn't walk a gerbil. His face suggested that he felt this was the indisputable argument-winner. One of the boys took a break from having his ear flicked to contribute that he didn't want to walk a gerbil because he'd look like a moron. At this point the mother decided that the conversation had gone on long enough and pointed out to her husband that they needed to concentrate on why they were here in the first place rather than talk about dogs. Since the reason they were there was essentially to wait, it was difficult to see how they could concentrate on that any more than by just sitting down.

Now here is the amazing part. From the moment that we entered the waiting room, we had to wait ten minutes to see the doctor. I'm so impressed about this that I'm going to repeat it again, except this time in capitals. TEN MINUTES! Now I'm of the slightly old-fashioned view that it is all right to wait four hours to see a highly skilled physician for free; one who is going to make you well when you are unwell; that this is actually OK rather than something to complain about endlessly. (Not a popular perspective when you live in a world where we are encouraged to think that if we can't get whatever we want yesterday then someone, somewhere needs a good sacking.) But ten minutes really was amazing.

So there we have it. Ten minutes and we had our daughter being examined by a really nice lady who wielded the ear thermometer like a third arm. Incredibly, she didn't bang it against a table or swear at it either. Damn, she was good. Anyway it turned out that my daughter's rash was nothing more than a cold (a not-unusual symptom of colds in very young babies is that they can be expressed through the skin rather than in the conventional adult manner of a runny nose).

Length of wait
TEN minutes. TEN.

Gregory House index (diagnostic capacity)
A cold and an ear infection were never going to tax most medical minds but still, she got it spot on.

Successful outcome?
Not only did we get seen in ten minutes by an efficient and hugely helpful doctor, but Anna was given some antibiotics for an ear infection, having been diagnosed straight away. I learned how to use an ear thermometer *and* I learned that you can't walk a gerbil. All free at the point of delivery.

Sympathetic and professional health care?
She was fantastic and even gave me a quick tutorial on how not to use the thermometer like it's your first time on earth. The little bastard no longer just bleeps at me intermittently when someone is ill. This means that I don't have to bash it against the table or be extremely rude to it. Everyone is happier with this new development.

Any signs of inefficiency and poor standards?
My attempts to wield the various thermometers that crossed my path were nothing short of an embarrassment, but the doctor didn't seem to share this disability.

Front page heading you won't find in the *Daily Mail*
'Man in out-of-hours clinic only has to wait ten minutes for treatment.'

The NHS 'how to look after a child in a day' course

The first response to the positive reading on the little pregnancy stick thingy is very often jubilation. If you are a normal human being, the second response is an expletive. This is not just because your life as you know it is going to be ripped apart with the vigour of a Christmas Day *EastEnders* special. It's not even because you find yourself sucked into a world of existential anxiety over your inherent suitability as a parent. For me it was principally because I had no idea whatsoever how to look after a baby. Up until that positive reading newborn babies had held all the appeal of a Ronan Keating cover version. 'Don't pass her to me — I'll probably just drop her on her face' had been quite effective at keeping the whole 'cuddling newborns' thing at arm's length. This had worked well until now. However, the side effect of this was that I was now clueless about these small creatures. Were I to write down a list of the things I knew about newborns, it would probably have looked at bit like this:

1. They cry a lot. This prompts everyone in the room to turn into budget Gina Fords and diagnose why. Teething, tiredness and

hunger seem to be big favourites. Not wanting to stand out I found that 'it's probably all the excitement' usually went unchallenged and allowed me to feel that I had contributed to this shared delusion of baby whispering.

2. They shit a lot. Be prepared with an answer that's better than 'Christ knows' if a guest asks what to do with their dirty nappy.

3. People talk about how beautiful they are and who they look most like despite the answer invariably being Clive Anderson.

4. They can't eat Hula Hoops. Once I was stuffing my face while holding a friend's baby and was beginning to feel a bit guilty, so I offered to give the baby one, too. I was genuinely quite taken aback by the sudden dash to take the baby back off me.

5. Unless they are yours they are pretty dull. They don't make any effort to contribute meaningfully to the conversation in the room and even have a tendency to make everyone talk about them.

6. Parents of new babies look like they are returning from a Middle East hostage crisis.

7. The stork brings them.

So, not too much really. But luckily the

NHS were on hand to help out here. I didn't know this in advance so was surprised when I got a letter through the door inviting us to an all-day event to help to prepare first-time parents. So my wife and I trotted along on our allotted day and it turned out to be superb. The atmosphere was relaxed, it was incredibly informative and completely devoid of the laborious one-upmanship that dogs NCT classes like a persistent stalker. It covered a wide array of topics including nappies, feeding, pain relief, maternity care, complications and so on. The classes were laid on at my local hospital for no money and so everyone had an opportunity to be there.

I was struck by a sense of amazement that in one day they could take a group of nervous, naïve and oblivious expectant parents and turn them into nervous, naïve and oblivious expectant parents who pretty much knew the basics of looking after a trainee human being. That's an educational feat up there with successfully teaching advanced algebra to a monkey that got all Ds and Es in monkey GCSEs — the kind of monkey that other sympathetic monkeys describe as being 'good with his hands'.

However, while the day was undoubtedly essential, what you didn't get was a guide in advance for how to behave on the day itself.

You see, if you really know nothing about birth and babies then knowing how to take care of them is only one half of the battle. What you also need to know are the things that are acceptable and indeed advisable to say and do when you take part in these days. Luckily I have made a list below for anyone who is a little unsure so that they can make the most out of their 'become a parent in a day' course.

Ten things to help you make the most of the NHS baby-prep days

1. Don't sit to the right or left of the demonstrating nurse. Hang back, see where she sits and then sit in the middle opposite her. Then, when she passes the plastic baby that needs bottle-feeding, you get to watch others mess it up like a car crash before it's your go. (Don't sit directly opposite, though, because then you might get the 'first in my eyeline' throw straight ahead, so sit just to the left or right of the middle of her.)

2. If you are a man don't talk about how it is your intention to share night feeds. Nobody believes you. And they are right.

3. If during one of the tea breaks you realize that the two men next to you are talking

about how they could beat Steve Redgrave in an arm wrestle, leave and go back for tea later.

4. Also, if you are a man, don't nod off. This is not interpreted as the action of a man who is tired and should be congratulated for making it along anyway. It will be understood as a man who is announcing to the world that 'none of this stuff is relevant to me, my wife will take care of it'. This plays about as well as saying 'we won't be needing any of this stuff' during the tour of the talks on pain-relief options.

5. Try not to pair up with hippies on the tour of the maternity area. They will ask loads of silly questions about having incense and mood music in the operating theatre should they require an emergency c-section. 'OK, the baby's heart rate is dropping, we are going to go straight to theatre. You page the anaesthetist but first can you page the odd bloke who sells incense sticks out the front of Primark? And tell him it's a goddamn emergency!'

6. If asked to write down on a piece of paper your three biggest anxieties about the birth process, don't write that your wife's labour pains might wake you up — it might get read out.

7. Don't make a joke of fetching some

chloroform to silence the crying doll that you are holding. People get a bit funny about men pretending to chloroform their own children.

8. If you see some complex but unknown mechanical equipment in the maternity suite, don't suggest to your wife that its purpose is to remove the mother's legs in the event of a difficult birth. Or at least not within earshot of others. It turns out that visits to maternity suites are quite tense affairs for some people.

9. Around four out of every ten men, when faced with a maternity room, will make the same joke about them needing gas and air, too. This will visibly crush with boredom any midwives in the vicinity. It is the equivalent of walking into a fruit and veg shop and putting a cucumber between your legs. Now, on the other hand, if you make the gas and air gag with a cucumber between your legs, that *is* different. You'll be ejected immediately but at least you've brought some originality to the table.

10. Apparently, things aren't that different for diabetic mums. I know this because after every single thing that anyone on the course said, a fatiguingly needy pregnant lady would ask, 'I'm diabetic so

will it be different for me?' As in:

Midwife:	'OK so when doing a nappy make sure you do up the straps firmly but not too firmly.'
Mrs Tedious:	'I'm diabetic so will it be different for me?'

By the end of the day our instructing midwife clearly wanted to scream, 'No, it bloody won't be different; now shut up!' But she didn't. A consummate professional.

Length of wait
No wait at all. In fact, we didn't even know it existed until the letter popped through our letterbox inviting us to attend a day. Following the Hula Hoop incident, I can't rule out that I was on some kind of special register of people who needed serious guidance should they ever decide to further populate the earth. Otherwise, I assume everyone gets this fantastic and essential opportunity.

Gregory House index (diagnostic capacity)
Not really applicable in this instance since the intervention was more preventative than diagnostic.

Successful outcome?
In one word, it was amazing. Almost everything that kept us afloat as we went through the parental L-plate months came from that single day. It also provided a handy justification to ignore the countless pieces of conflicting and usually unsolicited advice from various family members.

Sympathetic and professional health care?
The tone of the day was great. We had quite a wide variety of expectant parents on our course, from young to old, and including hippies, heavy metal fans and diabetics. They managed to deliver the course in a way that navigated the very different needs, expectations and desires of the people in the course. Apart from that diabetic woman. There needed to be a sign in the room saying 'maximum of five questions allowed about diabetes'.

Any signs of inefficiency and poor standards?
In all honesty I would probably have had a higher proportion of Bourbons to Rich Tea biscuits during the coffee breaks. If you are a greedy bastard who always tries to snaffle four or five biscuits when nobody is looking,

Rich Teas can get awfully dry by the fourth or fifth. Also, they could have included a bit more variety — perhaps with Hobnobs and custard creams — but other than that I think they got it spot on.

Front page heading you won't find in the _Daily Mail_
'The NHS can even make functioning parents out of men who think babies eat Hula Hoops.'

A quick guide to offending a sonographer

As with many areas of life, it is only when you see a job being performed badly that you come to fully appreciate what it looks like when it is being done well. Being a sonographer must be a pretty tough job. Nervous expectant parents come into your place of work and you have to engage in small talk while counting whether their future child has the right number of limbs and a heartbeat. It turns out that there are two ways you can do this. You can either do these checks as an internal monologue, or you can make them out loud. As a friend of mine found out, when sonographers decide to share their limb search process with parents, it's a pretty frightening few minutes.

'OK, there's one leg, and there are two legs . . . (pause) . . . and there's one arm and . . . (prolonged pause while parents try not to pass out in fear) . . . and there's the second one hiding, ha ha! Now let's see if we can find a heart and a brain.'

No person in the world wants to hear the phrase, 'Now let's see if we can find a heart and a brain.' It's up there with, 'I wouldn't worry, it's probably just cancer' and, 'Shall we watch that new Danny Dyer film?' in its sheer, unmitigated inappropriateness. If someone is trying to find out if my unborn child has a brain, I'm a little bit old-fashioned; I prefer just to hear the results rather than watch the search. I enjoy hide and seek as much as the next man, but always feel it works best if it's not a matter of life and death. I know, as I said, old-fashioned.

Anyway, as we sat in the waiting room for my son's scan I found myself hoping that we'd have one of the 'tell you the results at the end' types. And as I was looking around I was struck by a revelation. Having had my balls ultrasounded three times at that point, I had the epiphany that the same equipment in the same rooms did both foetal scans and testicle examinations. I wasn't certain about this and so I looked around the waiting room

144

to see if I could see any anxious men cupping their balls nestled in between the obviously pregnant women. I did actually see one but he was sat chatting to a pregnant woman so unless they were on a two-for-one ticket, it was likely that the ball-cupping was just incidental. Before I had a chance to test my theory, our names were called. It was our turn for baby-organ hide and seek.

The scan seemed to be going quite well, with us staring at an alien with a big head and trying to guess which parts of it looked human. I kept my eye on a white mass for long enough to have confidence that it was a leg; I then announced my finding and sat back, waiting for the impressed sonographer to congratulate me. She politely informed me that it was the umbilical cord, at which point I observed that they looked remarkably similar. Her eyes shot me a look that politely said 'No, they don't'. This was a bad start but I was pretty sure I could recover with a few humorous boasts about his size. I observed that he looked like he had the chest of a power lifter, just like his daddy. I felt like adding the caveat 'before I got the disco tits' but thought better of it.

It was at this point that I remembered that I was once told by my mum that I was initially a twin but that I ate the other twin inside the womb. Now, don't get me wrong, I'm a greedy shit but even I have standards. I don't eat dark chocolate because of its slightly bitter aftertaste so I hardly think I'd just rock up one day and eat a twin, regardless of how young I was. Anyway I felt a bit embarrassed about asking whether I could have eaten my twin so instead I just asked whether foetuses could eat things. Like heads and arms. It was at this point that I could see her make the inevitable decision to concentrate on just communicating with the person in the room who could competently tie their own shoelaces.

This was unfortunate because my wife subsequently had to leave the room to empty her bladder for the next round of shots. As Ruth disappeared I thought this was the perfect time to redeem myself with a sensible question. I told the sonographer about how I'd watched a programme where the scan only showed a single baby but that three babies popped out during birth. So, with this in mind, I asked if there was a chance that we might miss one hiding behind the liver or something? She pointed out that foetuses tend not to hide behind livers and that she was pretty sure that she would pick up a second child.

Suitably chastened, I stared at the ceiling

for a bit and waited for Ruth to come back but the silence was somewhat awkward. Now I have a little bit of a talent for filling awkward silences with even more awkward conversations (you may remember my testicle examination stories). In the past I have taken it upon myself to ask my friend what time his (painstakingly arranged surprise) birthday party was on Saturday. I have asked my friend's wife (who I hadn't previously met) how long they'd been married only to be told by what turned out to be his new girlfriend that they were now separated. I have asked a friend at university where he would be living now that he wasn't moving in with the three friends he'd previously arranged to move in with and he replied that to the best of his knowledge he was still moving in with them.

Now my policy whenever I find myself in that sort of situation is to immediately pretend to have stubbed my toe. OK, it's not great but it gives you a few extra seconds to try to effect a recovery and sometimes they even feel sorry for you.

Anyway, I didn't know it but here in this ultrasound room on a frosty Tuesday morning it turned out I was on that kind of form. I found myself asking whether, in her line of work, the sonographer ever came across expectant parents who were disappointed when she revealed the gender of their child. She replied that in fact this happened all the time and really wasn't uncommon. Now I have never really understood this mentality where you feel short-changed if you don't get one of each. I decided to share this with her. I told her that I thought that if you have the chance to have a child you should be thrilled whether it is a boy or a girl even if you have already had four of one sex. Any other attitude was deeply ungrateful, and felt a bit like a spoilt child crying on Christmas Day because that fat shit Santa gave him a toy truck rather than a new bike. I was really warming up to my topic and found myself calling such people absolutely pathetic. They should consider themselves lucky, I insisted, as there are people out there desperate for any child.

I have to say I felt quite unburdened after this and sat back in the full expectation of some praise from someone else who obviously understood that the miracle of life should not be reduced to the kind of mentality you have at a pic 'n' mix sweetie stall.

It was at that point that she stood up to reveal a clearly pregnant belly that had previously been hiding behind the bed and a loose examination jacket. Had I seen the bump beforehand, I'd probably have gone into my 'don't say anything controversial about pregnancy' mode (as I try not to make a habit of upsetting pregnant women). Sure enough, she replied that both she and her husband were disappointed with the news that they were having another girl as they had wanted one of each and this was likely to be their last child.

This was a code-red, stubbed-toe alert if I had ever seen one. Instincts kicked in and my feet felt around for something to stub my toe on, but there was nothing within a good six feet of my feet. Shit! I'd need to use another tactic. On account of the fact that she looked Asian, I found myself dredging up 'I suppose, though, that it is different in some cultures' before an alarm in my brain asked where I was going with this particular clanger. I think I had read in a magazine once that Indian men had a tendency to value male progeny over females. Even though I had no idea about the sonographer's background, *this* was what I had chosen to help me exclude her from my 'ungrateful parents' category. She politely replied that both she and her husband were British and that it wasn't really a cultural thing. Things were, at this stage, feeling pretty desperate. I have *never* wanted my wife to come out of a toilet more in my life, even when I have had a stomach upset where I was on the verge of explosion. In the space of two minutes I had achieved the following:

a) Upset a pregnant woman.
b) Insulted the father of her unborn child.
c) Implicated her in lazy and probably incorrect racial stereotypes.
d) Called her pathetic, spoilt and a number of other not particularly flattering things.

Nice going, even by my exalted standards. There was no possibility of talking my way out of this and nothing to stub my toe on (I checked again). So I thought, 'Let's concentrate on the matter in hand — what we came in for — and let's focus on our unborn baby,' so I looked up at the screens to try to divert myself from the sorry mess I was in. I noticed the screen was blank and can only assume that I was too flustered to think straight as I asked her if we could have another look at the little one while we were waiting for my wife to return. She pointed out that the screen was blank because the little one and her mother were currently sitting in the toilet. So to my list above I added:

e) Identified myself as someone who thought

that you could do an ultrasound of a baby without the baby being there.

After this, I decided that it was best to sit in silence until my wife came in a few seconds later. For the rest of the consultation I kept my observations to myself and found that when I did this it seemed to go much better.

Length of wait
Twenty-five minutes.

Gregory House index (diagnostic capacity)
She was there to determine whether my son was a healthy foetus. She did this with ease and, as outlined above, managed to do it with sensitivity and professionalism, even when she was asked to look at the foetus on the ultrasound machine when it wasn't actually in the room.

Successful outcome?
We went in hoping to be told that our unborn child was fine and following a very relaxing and informed examination, left with the information that our unborn child was fine. As good as it gets.

Sympathetic and professional health

care?

Even under these circumstances, our sonographer responded with professionalism and patience. Overall, the session was sensitively handled (she decided to go for the 'counting limbs in your head' method), and she handled our questions and anxieties really well. Despite my essentially insulting both her and her husband she managed to be really nice and civil to me. She was gentle in the way that she moved Ruth and our baby into position, talked us through what she was doing, what measures she was taking and why, and was constantly reassuring, asking if we had any questions. In short, she performed the dual role of performing an array of technical medical examinations and managing the anxiety of expectant parents with real dexterity and poise, especially bearing in mind some of the questions she was having thrown at her.

Any signs of inefficiency and poor standards?

Only in the patient (although my views on people who are picky about the sex of their child haven't changed).

Front page heading you won't find in the *Daily Mail*

'Sensitive sonographer makes nerve-racking scan a bit less nerve-racking.'

Coca Cola does physiotherapy

I decided, back in 1998, for reasons that I still don't fully understand, to have a go at the London Marathon. I liked jogging, I lived in London and I had some free time on my hands. And surprisingly it went OK. I lost my shorts on the day (not while I was running I might add) just before breakfast-time; all I could find to wear were some old Bermuda shorts so I didn't look great but I got to the end. I was aware that they take your photo as you cross the line so I tried to compose myself, raised my hands in triumph and waited patiently for the picture of my crowning glory to arrive in the post.

And it did. Sure enough, there I was, a sweaty bundle of exhausted satisfaction, with my arms raised in the air. Moreover, there was someone next to me, or rather, I should say, just in front of me. Another athlete had just pipped me to the post and, frankly, she didn't really look that tired — more like she had just been out for an afternoon stroll along the Mall. And this woman was *old*. I mean proper old. She looked like Old Father

Time's oldest Gran. And she had beaten me in a marathon. Comfortably. And, if you looked carefully, you could see she was looking across at me with a gentle smile that said 'I was born before your great-granddad and I still beat you, you fat shit.' She might not have said the words, but it was all in the eyes.

This left me with two options. I could either cut out her face and replace it with Mo Farah's and hope nobody asked why Mo Farah had white wrinkly legs. Or I could do the marathon again and get a clean photo unsullied by Barbara Cartland's mum. So, roll on some years later (it didn't bother me that much) and I started training again. I took it quite seriously too: loads of hill running; loads of miles; I even cut down my cheese McCoys daily intake from four packets to three and gave up fags. Yup, I was serious this time.

And then a potential travesty occurred that looked like it might derail my attempts to redeem my running self-esteem. I was struck down by injury three weeks before the big event. I woke up one morning and the sole of my right foot was in such pain that I couldn't put my foot down. This was bad. Really bad. So I went to see my doctor. I couldn't imagine that there was much I could do to get it right in the short time between then and the start of the race, but thought I'd give it a try. I was expecting to be told the usual. Rest, anti-inflammatories and maybe some exercises to do for recovery. Instead, my GP gave the following advice: 'Just get a cold can of Coke, and roll on top of it ten times, three times day — the pain'll be gone in a few days.'

I stared at her in disbelief. 'A Coke can?'

'Yup, or any other can of drink, really.' A few seconds passed in silence as I stared at her and tried to comprehend what I had just heard. Then she added, 'And you might want to put a sock on it as it can get very cold. A nice fluffy one, ideally.'

OK, Carl, let's think straight here. Occam's razor — the simplest explanation is usually the correct one. *Beadle's About*. It's got to be. There were two problems with this explanation. Number one, there weren't any cameras, concealed or otherwise. Number two, and probably more problematic, was the fact that Jeremy Beadle was dead. Beadle was a good practical joker, but he wasn't so good that he could return from beyond the grave to stitch a person up.

So once I had discounted Beadle, I went through the remaining possible options and realized that the only reasonable explanation was that this person clearly wasn't a doctor. Whatever else she was, she was *not* a doctor. Doctors tell you to rest and take ibuprofen, not to roll on cans of soft drink. The question was, who was she? She was wearing a white coat but surely no doctors wore white coats these days. I had the uncomfortable thought that the only person who would wear a white coat was someone who was *pretending* to be a doctor. I was reminded of a story in America where someone walked in off the street with a white coat and started practising medicine. Didn't get found out for months, apparently. Maybe that was what was happening here?

I looked around the room casually to see if there was a cupboard where the real doctor might be, bound and trussed. No cupboards. Time to take the direct approach.

'Er, don't take this the wrong way, but that's an odd recommendation for a doctor to make.' I didn't really hear what she said next as I was trying to figure out whether I could call the police with my phone in my pocket. My fingers felt across the keyboard, but my trousers were too tight to get any purchase on the keys. If she made a move, it was just me and her. I checked her desk to see if there were any sharp implements. Just a blood pressure machine and a diary. It was going to be hand to hand.

'A Coke can?' I repeated. I needed to buy myself some time as I edged towards the door.

'You look confused, Mr Walker.'

'No, not at all. Not confused at all. I'm right on message with this, right on message.' I felt for my phone again.

'You have plantar fasciitis. It's an inflammation of the connective tissue on the sole of the foot, often brought on by hill running.'

Shit, she's talking like a doctor again. What now? OK, stay focused, Carl. Don't let her draw you in. Anyone can look up a few medical terms. Keep your eyes on the prize here.

'The Coke can is a form of cold therapy; it helps to reduce the pain and swelling.'

Shit. That sort of made sense. Maybe she was a real doctor after all? Slightly embarrassed, I let out a deep breath, thanked her and left the office.

Length of wait
Thirty minutes.

Gregory House index (diagnostic capacity)
Spot on. Owing to some good diagnostic

157

work I was able to complete my marathon and get the photo that I needed.

Successful outcome?
Amazingly, yes. From being barely able to walk, after four to five days I was pain-free and ready to resume light training.

Sympathetic and professional health care?
Yes. She was nice, even through the trauma of being treated like she was in the middle of a debilitating psychosis.

Any signs of inefficiency and poor standards?
Not in the slightest.

Front page heading you won't find in the *Daily Mail*
'Quick diagnosis and creative thinking lets marathon man erase the ghost of world's oldest woman.'

Beating the medical bouncers

GPs have long been regarded as the gatekeepers of the NHS, responsible for the delicate task of juggling the clinical needs of individual patients with the general health of the wider population. If patients need to be seen by a hospital doctor, they generally have to be referred by a GP. The problem is that in the twenty-first century, with a well-educated population and the internet to hand, much of the mystique has been wrenched from medicine. Quite often when you go along to your doctor's you have an idea of what is wrong with you and what you need to remedy it. Sometimes you're wrong; often you're right.

On the occasions when you know what is wrong with you and what needs to be done about it, I find it useful to conceptualize primary care health professionals as being a little bit like bouncers. Sure, they don't wear black leather bomber jackets or prioritize pretty girls with short skirts for treatment. But in other respects they function pretty much like bouncers. In these circumstances patients are no longer patients but health hustlers, intent on flattering, exaggerating and jostling their beleaguered health professional into a specific course of action. If you want to hustle your way into a nightclub, you hide your trainers, speak slowly to disguise the obvious slurring, and try to look like you're not the kind of person who is going to eject a cocktail of drinks that you couldn't handle into the middle of their dance floor.

With the GP it's OK to look like you're going to throw up. They don't tend to mind that. They don't really mind trainers either and you don't have to pair up with a pretty girl to be treated equitably. But sometimes you have to hustle them. There are big hustles (gastric band, gender reassignment surgery) and there are small hustles (getting antibiotics and stronger painkillers), but they all essentially require a hustle. The problem is, of course, that the role of the GP is not to be hustled into courses of action, but to assess correctly the medical needs of the patient.

My tonsils have led me into my fair share of hustling over the years and, during these years, I have learned something about tonsils — namely, that they are complete bastards. That probably seems like an absurd statement to many people. If you look at a medical textbook it'll tell you that the term (tonsils, not bastards) most commonly refers specifically to the palatine tonsils, which are masses of lymphatic material situated at either side at the back of the human throat. It'll further tell you that the palatine tonsils and the nasopharyngeal tonsil are lymphoepithelial tissues located near the oropharynx and nasopharynx and that these immunocompetent tissues are the immune system's first line of defence against ingested or inhaled foreign pathogens. It might also say that the fundamental immunological roles of tonsils have yet to be understood.

But this is utter bollocks. The tonsils have a specific and clear role and anyone with a set of active tonsils knows what this is. Their role is to sit diligently at the back of your throat completely dormant and forgotten until you have a social event that you've been looking forward to for weeks — at which point their job is to flare up and screw you over. Just as you are getting yourself prepared, getting a new shirt for the event, talking excitedly to friends in preparation, your tonsils are doing the same, checking out their new look in the mirror for *their* big event.

How do they do this? It's simple. They can think. That's right: tonsils have agency; they make decisions. Someone once said in a film that the best trick the devil played on human beings was convincing them that he didn't exist. I feel the same about tonsils. Everyone thinks they are just body parts like any other and that's exactly what they want you to think. But think like that and you've already lost the battle. And I can prove it.

Now, like a few particularly unlucky adults, my tonsils are aggressive little bastards. You just have to look at them the wrong way and they'll flare up into giant mouth testicles. They really don't need too many invitations. So I should just get them taken out, right? The problem is that there is a gatekeeping policy for being able to access that particular medical procedure. If you don't have tonsillitis on at least five separate occasions in a calendar year, you ain't coming in. The bouncers don't want to know. Now, my tonsils know this. Even though my mouth is shut during consultations, these little bastards have heard every word and have a little calendar of their own. I know they know this because they will flare up four times in a calendar year and then go dormant until the start of the next calendar year. After that fourth time I could try to break the world record for French-kissing dogs with rabies and I still wouldn't get another bout. No, sir; they bed down and go to sleep until after the New Year.

Because of this I have had to do a spot of medical hustling. I can't tell the GP that my tonsils will never flare up five times in a calendar year because they are too smart for that, or else I'll probably find myself being referred for an altogether different kind of medical issue. Once I hit four for the year I have to convince them to break the five times rule. I have to tell them that the tonsillitis is so debilitating and severe that they need to come out.

So there I am with tonsillitis bout number four. If I listen carefully I can hear them chuckling away as they block up my throat with their mass of white pussiness. I'm feeling like shit, high temperature, in pain but I have to focus, keep a clear head. I'm going to go in and fight the good fight with Jenny, the nurse practitioner who deals with people with routine everyday infections. Jenny knows me: we've had this conversation before, and she's bounced me right out of the surgery with a prescription and an apologetic manner.

But not today. I look at myself in the mirror, slap myself in the face a few times to perk myself up for the battle of wills ahead. My chins wobble more than they should at this, so I stop. I tell myself to be strong. I can hear the *Rocky* theme playing in my head. I practise my hustle. Got to get it right this time, got to get out of the surgery with a referral to an ENT surgeon. I need to finally consign these little shits to history. In the past, Jenny has always managed to find a way to convince me that they don't need to go. Usually by mentioning how much they bleed. I hate blood and am an utter coward and I think she knows this. This time, I tell myself that, whatever she says, I shouldn't let her get to me. Be prepared; tell her that I'm OK with the bleeding stuff. On this occasion I have had four bouts of tonsillitis between January and early March. I am ready to have them out. Jenny is a lovely woman as well as a great medic; but I have to put that out of my mind. Today she is the enemy.

So I sit in the surgery waiting room practising my 'engulfed in suffering' look. I mean, they are sore but I need to lay this on thick. 'A bit sore' isn't going to cut it. I look around to see if there is anyone in obvious agony who can provide me with inspiration, but I only see a woman with a toddler whose uneasy focus on me suggests that he knows something terrible about me that I don't. These two are going to be useless. What I need for inspiration is a hypochondriac who is genuinely ill. Nobody does suffering better than these people. But today I am out of luck.

'Hi, Carl, is it the tonsils again?' Her tone is perky and unconcerned, a tone of voice that screams 'no surgical referral today for you, my friend'. First blood to her.

'Yeah, they're really bad again,' I say, looking deeply sorry for myself and giving a sickly little cough to show how unwell I am.

'Well, let's take a look then.' She takes a look. 'Oh, yes, they are big again. Any other symptoms? Fever?'

'Yes, I've had a temperature. A very high one, really very high.'

'Right, how high?'

'Er, not sure, I didn't measure it, but it was very high. You could have fried an egg on my forehead.'

No! Idiot! People who need to be referred for surgery don't make jokes about frying eggs on their heads. Get a grip here or this will be over in minutes. Two nil to her. 'It's my fourth bout in the last few months; it's just getting too much now.'

Jenny checks the computer. 'I only have it down as three.'

'No, it's four because I had it twice last time.'

'Were you ever really properly better between these two bouts?'

'Er, yeah, I was fine.' This is obviously a lie. If we were playing chess right now my queen would be under serious attack. Time to pull out the trump card. 'But my tonsils don't know that.' Shit, that sounds less like a trump card than I thought it would.

'Sorry?'

Right, time to go for the kill. I need to set out my three key moves to take her king (can't eat, can't sleep, can't breathe properly). 'I can't eat properly with these bouts; it's terrible.' She looked over my body, and I

165

swear her eyes were saying, 'Yeah, but you'll hardly starve, will you?' Still, I persisted. 'I can't breathe properly and it disrupts my sleep terribly.'

'Are you really struggling to breathe with them?'

'Well, er, a bit.' Dammit she's got me again.

Then she uses her big guns, she sits back in her seat. Go on, Jenny, hit me with the best you've got, I'm ready this time. 'Look, I know you'd like them out but it's a very dangerous operation for adults, the tonsils are close to a great many arteries and the danger of big bleeds is very real.' Shit, she's done it again, instilled images of me bleeding to death in my sleep from a tonsil-less hole. But this time I'm ready to fight fire with fire.

'Ah, but what about if they are already bleeding?' That's put her right on the back foot. Two-one.

'Are they already bleeding?'

'Er . . . they might be.' Hmm, not really thought this through. Just lost my bishop.

'Have you seen any evidence of blood?'

'Well, no.' Bollocks, there goes a rook. She's officially back on the front foot.

'Abnormal bleeding is more common in adults than in children. According to experts one in five adults has a bleed that won't stop.' That won't stop? I'm beginning to feel a bit queasy. 'Bleeding can arise within twenty-four hours and last as long as a week after the operation. Additional surgery may be necessary to control the bleeding.' Stop mentioning bleeding, woman! Just stop it, for God's sake! My king is wobbling here. 'Occasionally, the bleeding may be so severe that a blood transfusion is needed.' Boom, the king falls.

'Right, well, I guess I'll just have some antibiotics then.' I could make out the faint noise of my tonsils laughing at me from inside my throat. 'Better luck next time, fatty.'

Next time, Jenny, next time.

Length of wait
Disappointingly it was around five minutes. Nowhere near long enough for me to be inspired into the correct mindset of agonizing self-pity by my fellow patients.

Gregory House index (diagnostic capacity)
Any complex surgery for a recurring health issue involves balancing quality of life with risk of surgical complications. Hence the criteria of five before surgery is considered. Jenny knows me and, more importantly, she knows my tonsils. She knew I hadn't met the criteria and sent me packing. And she was probably right, even if I did sulk all the way

home like a child who'd had a turd slipped into their ice cream when they weren't looking.

Successful outcome?
Yes and no. 'Yes' in that I was given the correct diagnosis and treatment. As I always am. 'No' in that the correct diagnosis was not the one that I wanted. However, since the tonsils have calmed down a bit in recent years I am grudgingly coming round to the view that Jenny, and the entire educated medical establishment, were probably right on this one.

Sympathetic and professional health care?
As always, excellent. She was friendly, polite and knowledgeable and one shouldn't under-estimate the opening line that shows she remembers you when you walk through the door. The idea that a medical professional somewhere knows you and your history is nice.

Any signs of inefficiency and poor standards?
Inefficiency and poor standards would have allowed me to be referred for an operation that I didn't, on the balance of things, need.

Sadly, in this case the standards were high and efficiency wasn't compromised. Perhaps next time I need to catch an inexperienced young locum on the hop.

Front page heading you won't find in the *Daily Mail*
'Nurse practitioner correctly convinces patient that he doesn't need complicated surgery.'

Dealing with idiots 2: the back spot

While it is clear that the role of the variety of health practitioners in the NHS is to help to identify and treat illness, it is also a key part of their role to identify those who *don't* need help. An example of just such an instance originated for me with a walk in the local park. It was a Saturday morning and part of my daddy daycare routine at the time involved taking my daughter and baby son to the park for a stroll. Now it is not uncommon to bump into other fathers with children on these weekend mornings, and occasionally you share a passing hello and an 'I love spending time with my kids but I want to be in bed sleeping' look, somewhere between a smile and a knowing grimace.

There was one particular father whose

routine seemed to cross with mine. When I first saw him I was taken aback by just how manically excited he looked to be part of the daddy morning club. In fact he looked so excited that he had gone beyond the 'I'm so proud to be a dad to my beautiful child' club and was lingering on the boundaries of the 'I'm not well and I've stolen a baby so that I can be part of the daddy club' fraternity. Every week he looked like he had just won the lottery; so much so that it prompted me to do an internet search on 'stolen babies in Worthing'. Nothing came up so I felt a bit ashamed. I made a point of saying 'hello' to him next time I saw him to help assuage my guilt.

And then I didn't see him for ages. Maybe a full eighteen months went by with no manically excited daddy pushing his bright green pram. I figured that he'd been sprung and had to give back the baby. Until one day he reappeared, complete once again with a manic look of self-satisfaction. The problem was that he was pushing the same baby pram. And it was a very small baby pram. His child by now would have been over eighteen months old and clearly too big for that pram. Most probably they would have been toddling around. If he'd had another child in the interim then he would have had a little toddler with him. It was then that it dawned on me that the problem wasn't that he had stolen a child but that he'd *never had a child in the first place*. I started trying to sneak a look. I tried from all angles but it wasn't happening. Either he was very adept at hiding fake babies after eighteen months of practice or I need more practice at the art of identifying fake babies.

One morning he caught me using the cover of a game of hide and seek with the kids to catch a look and he said 'hello'. We got chatting and I have to say he didn't come across as a man with a fake/stolen baby (although, to be fair, I'm not sure what conversational characteristics would have rendered him an appropriate candidate for fake baby pusher). He saw me scratching my back and asked if I was OK. I told him that I'd had a spot there for a while and it was getting on my nerves. I figured this would be the end of that line of conversation but oh, no. Not even close. He went on to tell me that he had a friend who used to be a roadie for Tears for Fears, who had had a little spot on his back. 'Six weeks later he was as dead as a dormouse. Died in agony, a slow, slow death. He scratched his back, too.'

Of course, it crossed my mind that he may be exacting a cold, calculated revenge for my pram investigations. But a confirmed hypochondriac can't hear that kind of story without descending into a spiral of serious reflection. I thought about it for the rest of the day. Yes, it had come from a man who might have a fake/stolen baby but I was still going to have to check it out. I asked my brother whether he thought it was cancerous but his answer of 'How the fuck should I know?' wasn't sufficiently medical to put the matter to rest.

So there I was staring at a locum GP. I was preparing myself for the worst. To be told that it was the Big C. I'd looked at the internet to find out whether a spot could be cancerous. After five minutes of reading I was divvying up my possessions.

'What is it, doctor? Be straight with me.'

'It's a spot.'

'I know that, doctor, but is it bad? Is it a bad spot?'

'No, it's just a spot.'

'Just a spot?'

'Yup.'

'Oh . . . not cancer?'

'Nope, not cancer.'

I won't lie, I was feeling like a bit of an idiot at this point. So I did what any self-respecting moral coward would do and blamed someone else. 'Well, of course, I didn't think it was anything, either. It's just that this bloke from the park had a mate who used to be a roadie for Tears for Fears had a spot and then he was dead within three weeks.' (At this stage, why not exaggerate?)

'Tears for Fears?'

'Apparently, although I'd take what he says with a pinch of salt, I'm not even sure there's a baby in his pram.'

'Right.'

'Anyway, I'm really sorry to waste your time, I knew it was a silly idea.'

'No, you were right to get it checked out. You should always get things checked out if you are worried. It's always better to be safe than sorry, so well done for that.'

'Right. Thanks, doctor, bye.'

Length of wait
Twenty minutes.

Gregory House index (diagnostic capacity)
She spotted that a spot was . . . a spot. At the end of her career this realization is unlikely to play a prominent part in any bid she might make for the Nobel Prize for medicine.

Successful outcome?
I went in with nothing wrong with me and

left with nothing wrong with me. I suppose that has to be a yes.

Sympathetic and professional health care?

The locum GP was really nice. In front of her sat a hypochondriac who was throwing around accusations of fake babies, pretending someone else told him to come to the doctor's and who had fundamentally wasted her time, but she still managed to find something to congratulate me for.

Any signs of inefficiency and poor standards?

Bearing in mind that Brian Harvey from the band East 17, a man who managed to run himself over, citing a bellyful of jacket potatoes as the cause, is probably over-qualified to make this diagnosis, it's not the best one to use for judging efficiency and standards.

Front page heading you won't find in the *Daily Mail*

'Doctor manages not to laugh at man whose spot is a spot.'

(P.S. I never did find out the truth about the pram man.)

The Saturday night shift

When I was younger and still living at home, I returned one night with my friend Paul to hear my mother excitedly tell me that my younger brother had been taken to hospital after a night out. Apparently, he had had an allergic reaction of some sort — although, when we turned up at the hospital and found our way to his bed, we realized that his allergic reaction had been to ten pints of lager. This impression was confirmed by his friend Pete, who was sitting next to him looking like he'd drunk so much that he'd almost forgotten how to breathe. As mothers do, my mother was hanging onto the whole 'allergic reaction' thing, but the doctors had spotted that tell-tale sign of heavy drinking — the fact that he was unequivocally bladdered.

However, my brother's travails are not the focus of this piece. Rather, it was what I saw when I surveyed the Saturday night ward that proved utterly captivating in its shocking grimness. The people who filled this ward were all casualties of the illness better known as 'British Saturday night out disease'. And it was a truly harrowing sight. As I looked around me I was suddenly mindful of Florence Nightingale walking the wards of her Crimean field hospital, tending to wounded soldiers. There is no better phrase that describes the ward that night than to say that it was an utter warzone. There were people puking in their beds, puking on the floor, puking down their tops. It was like I had stumbled into an international food-poisoning contest.

And from what I could see, there wasn't really a great deal of medicine happening. I remember thinking how well the doctors and nurses handled the often hideously drunk patients, as well as their friends and families whose stock line seemed to be 'But he only had a couple of pints; he can normally handle his drink!' I suppose my brother and Pete should be given credit for plumping for the altogether more innovative 'allergy' angle.

I watched a nurse as she moved around the ward. She came first to an old man repeatedly complaining that his arse had fallen through. Now I am no medic, but I did a little bit of investigating myself (I tilted my head) and I could see no sign of an arse on the floor under his bed. A junior doctor came along with a stethoscope at the ready. I silently praised the old man because he was considerably less distressed than I would have been had I lost *my* arse. While being treated, the old man with the imaginary prolapse was told repeatedly by the man in the next bed that he wouldn't last a 'single fucking moment in Afghanistan'.

Now this man was huge. On his arm was a tattoo, seemingly drawn by a tattoo artist with advanced Parkinson's. It looked like a dragon fucking a stripper, although it was difficult to tell. He was also letting everyone know that he needed a piss. This man was being placated by his partner and told to calm down. He replied that he didn't want anyone lairing him up because he didn't need the grief. One assumes that the old man in question was lairing him up via the medium of a suspected anal collapse. I know that whenever I want to be aggressive to somebody, the first thing I do is not insult them or hit them but to prolapse.

Now this tattooed man was next in the queue. Me personally? I would have avoided his bed like it had a sign saying 'get your dose of the clap here,' but the junior doctor went straight over, calmed him down and inspected his potentially broken jaw. To be fair, the tattooed man then apologized and calmed down. He shared with the doctor the results of his own medical inspection, which (like mine) suggested that the old man was a timewaster who hadn't actually lost his arse.

In addition to these characters, there was a

woman loudly reiterating that she needed her appendix taken out. However, she appeared to be holding her leg, so either there was a misidentification of the symptoms or she had the biggest appendix in history. She eventually threw up on her bed, at which point her two friends broached the subject that her appendix might not be the problem.

There was also a little skinny man who said to the doctor, 'Oi, you! Don't give me no lip.' He looked like an anorexic Ross Kemp after an attempt to eat a lawn-mower. His face was covered with blood. Now, he had obviously reflected on the various options he had at his disposal to address his ailment and decided that threatening to punch the doctor in the face, via the medium of a messy double negative, was the optimal solution. When asked to calm down by his partner/mother/both (she looked a lot like him), he reminded her that he wasn't 'taking no fucking jip off nobody'. He felt this point so strongly that he repeated it loudly so that everyone in the ward could hear — I guess, in case some of them were in the process of procuring him some jip. 'Ssh, they'll get security,' he was told by his female companion. 'Get them. I'll slap them up, too.' You had to hand it to this guy — he really knew how to make hospital work for him.

Finally, there was a perfectly friendly man whose ailment was not visible but who was telling the nurse that he thought he'd had something stolen from him. His friend was telling him that he had already lost it when they were in the club, but he countered this by saying this was impossible because he sat in the same seat he always had. This bout of irrefutable logic was like a slap in the face to his friend, who just sat down and played with his balls.

Like I said, a warzone.

I suspect that my little brother was on the 'people with nothing wrong with them' list in the nurses' station and so I had some time to wait before a doctor made his way round to our corner of the ward. For our part my mother was repeatedly and loudly telling anyone who would listen that they weren't doing their job properly because allergies can kill people. That my little brother couldn't have looked more pissed if he had a yard of ale clasped in his arms seemed to cut no ice. Still, at least it meant that we weren't letting the side down by not complaining about how people weren't doing their jobs properly.

The doctors and nurses made their way around this merry lot: calming people down; convincing them that their appendix was not in their legs; assuring them that their arse was just where they left it; and, of course, fixing them up. I watched them go from bed to bed. They were facing aggression, inebriation, senselessness, incoherence and frantic friends and families, who were often drunk themselves. All the while they were having their professional integrity questioned both regularly and loudly. This was a tough shift. And it took its toll. They could be sullen, occasionally monosyllabic and it looked like, whenever possible, they would hang on for just that few seconds extra in the nurses' station before they came back to the bear pit. But come back they did. And despite it all, they patched these people up and sent them on their way. In few other walks of life do we work with people who are off their tits. Bars won't sell alcohol to them; bouncers won't let them into clubs; taxis reserve the right not to take them — but the hospitals? Hospitals *always* open their doors. And it makes for a tough working environment. From what I could see, the staff were doing their best. I'm pretty sure that even the Lady with the Lamp would have disappeared when faced with this lot.

(By the way it seems that 'allergy' is still the official line at family reunions.)

Length of wait
About two hours — which may seem like a

long time, but when there's nothing wrong with you, and there's loads of other people who have essentially nothing wrong with them to get through, it's not too bad.

Gregory House index (diagnostic capacity)

They spotted that my brother was legless and had passed out. Not their toughest gig of the evening.

Successful outcome?

My brother went in there pissed and passed out. He left there pissed and no longer passed out. What miracle of modern medical science made this happen for us? Was it the MRI? The EEG? Nope, he just lay on a hospital bed and slept it off for a couple of hours. Thank God this happened in 2013.

Sympathetic and professional health care?

As much as could be expected, given the circumstances. I wouldn't have felt comfortable doing a round on that ward without at least a flamethrower by my side.

Any signs of inefficiency and poor standards?

British A&E wards on a Saturday night are

less about efficiency and standards, and more about survival.

Front page heading you won't find in the *Daily Mail*

'Junior doctors and nurses help vulnerable people with self-inflicted wounds feel better while avoiding violence, threats and vomit very late on a Saturday night when everyone else who complains about 'the bloody NHS' is in bed.' (A bit wordy but you get the gist.)

The problem of novices trying out medicine: my mate's ingrowing toenail

In the UK we don't have to worry about health insurance. This is because our National Health Service is free at the point of delivery of care. However, the giant leap toward privatization inherent in the provisions of the 2012 Health and Social Care Act will eventually change that. This is the health care model that our cousins in the US have decided to adopt and, if you are sufficiently wealthy or lucky enough to have a job that brings health care coverage, then you no doubt think it's superb.

The problem is that the proportion of Americans with health insurance has been steadily declining since at least 2000. This is not because the turn of the century saw the realization of NASA's project to make superpeople who didn't need health care. It's because, owing to a general trend toward stagnating wages and rising living costs similar to that in the UK, everybody is skint. As of 2014 more than 50 million Americans do not have any form of health insurance. And that's a lot of people who are screwed if they get ill or injured.[5]

Since people who lack health insurance are unable to obtain timely medical care, they have a 40% higher risk of death in any given year than those with health insurance. A study in the *American Journal of Public Health*[6] estimated that in 2005 in the United States, there were 45,000 deaths associated with lack of health insurance. I suppose you could say that on the plus side that's 45,000 people who don't have to worry about health insurance any more, but that feels a little bit like scraping the 'positives' barrel.

So what do the 50 million do when they become ill and injured? Well, they do what you and I would do, of course: they try to fix themselves. A little bit like when your washing machine stops working and you want to save hundreds of pounds on an engineer, you grab your tools, get on the internet and have a go yourself. Of course, nine times out of ten you mess it up, but that's OK — it was worth a try. In America, a similar 'washing machine' approach is being put to work on livers and femurs and pancreases. People are borrowing leftover prescription drugs from friends, stretching their diabetes and asthma medicines for as long as possible and setting their own broken bones. People with urinary tract infections are taking medications far better suited for ear infections or pneumonia. This isn't because they don't know the difference between a urinary tract and an ear. It's because they have no money to buy the correct medications.

So what are the consequences of this turn of events? Well, it just so happens that I have a perfect example of what occurs when medically naïve but reasonably well-educated people take on the responsibility of fixing a health care issue. Let's see how it worked out.

Twenty years or so ago when I was a student a few of us went to visit my friend Paul. We were drinking in a local pub when, following a particularly painful toe stubbing against the pool table, Paul revealed that he had an ingrowing toenail. Despite the best efforts of chiropodists, it kept growing back after being repeatedly removed. He said that it was probably infected and was causing him great distress. Paul made an alcohol-filled request that I suspect he came to regret. He asked whether, once we got back to the flat, one of us could yank it off for him. He'd seen it done many times by the chiropodist and didn't want to wait because he was in a lot of discomfort.

In the taxi back to his digs we thought about it. Sure, we'd been power-drinking; sure we had no medical experience whatsoever; sure we had no appropriate tools to take it out with; sure we were nowhere near a doctor if things went wrong, but, seriously, how hard could it be? If Charlie Fairhead from *Casualty* could do it, then so could we.

So who did we have on our medical team? Well, a pretty highly trained bunch as it happened. We had Dr Kevin Jaggs, twenty-two, who brought his skills in petroleum geophysics into the equation — a much needed skillset when you are yanking off a toenail. We had Dr Neil Johnson, a chemistry student who once saw his nan pull a toenail off. (That kind of experience was going to be priceless so he would be our intellectual 'go-to' guy for the operation.) We had myself, a zoology student. (Animals have toes too, although at the time I couldn't think of any with toenails. Not to worry.) We had Dr Nicola Tait, a civil engineering student whose knowledge of the structural dynamics of bridges and big things might just be invaluable if we could wake her up from what looked like a Bacardi coma.) And finally we had our doubting Thomas, Dr Ruth Atkinson, a theatre studies and English student who told us we were idiots for even thinking of trying this. She clearly wasn't a medical person like the rest of us so we took this with a pinch of salt. I had done an afternoon first aid course when I was in the air cadets as a child, so this made me the consultant chiropodist. In the land of the blind and all that.

While we were drunk, we still had the wherewithal to carry out a risk assessment. This involved thinking about what would happen if we irreparably screwed up the toe. Somebody (Dr Johnson, I believe) said that you can't walk without your big toes. Apparently, they are essential for balance. This sounded like important information that we needed to incorporate. So a few of us did an ad hoc experiment where we walked along but with our big toes sticking up in the air. This proved to be difficult. Someone said we needed some string to tie to our big toes so that we could pull them up with our hands as we walked, a bit like a puppeteer. We couldn't find any string so we just gave it a go as it was. We did fall over but that was probably the Bacardi, not the toes. OK, if the worst came to the worst and we lost the toe, Paul could still walk. Risk assessment section 2 — I needed to figure out if I was going to puke during the operation. Probably not standard NHS practice, but then they weren't usually wrestling with a kebab that hadn't really settled.

Finally, our medical team convened for a conversation about the toe and to see if we could source any more booze. It was pointed out by Neil that tonsils have loads of arteries around them. Kev confirmed that we'd be OK because you don't have tonsils on your toes. However, Neil's point had been that there may be arteries around the big toe that we didn't know about. This was before the internet age so we were on our own on this. Someone said that we didn't have to worry because there were no veins or arteries in the feet. Nobody believed this, but we needed reassurance so we went with it. We were satisfied that we could proceed.

Now we needed some tools for the job. As Neil went off to find our medical kit, the medical team reflected that big toes might actually be vestigial structures. That is, structures that have no actual use to the human body (like the appendix). 'Yeah and the pancreas,' someone else chimed in. 'I mean, what does the pancreas actually do?' It needed to be pointed out at this stage by the chief consultant (me) that we ought not to confuse our not knowing what a body part did, with it having no actual use to humans. Someone suggested that we could really move science on here. Forget the toenail, we could pull off all of the toes to see if they were vestigial. Paul wasn't excited about the direction his medical team were taking in this conversation and asked us to focus on the task in hand.

Neil came running back excitedly with a hammer. 'I found this, guys!' It was not clear whether he had intended this to be a particularly brutal form of anaesthesia or a means of smashing the toenail and toe off with brute force. Either way, Paul thought it prudent to use his veto at this point. He had been thinking of a more subtle instrument. Somebody suggested pliers and this seemed like a really good idea to everyone. I think that the person who suggested this won considerable praise for their medical ingenuity. Neil then found some pliers in an old toolbox and everyone agreed that this was a far better medical instrument. We checked once more for consent as we suspected that the sight of these tools might have prompted a reappraisal from our patient. But, no, our patient was still very much with us, repeatedly saying, 'Don't piss around: just do it!'

Kevin then came into the room and gleefully announced that he'd found some Listerine mouthwash. His place on our elite medical team was suddenly thrown into doubt. After all, bad breath wasn't really part of the differential. But he won us around by saying that Listerine might act as an antiseptic for the toe to stop it getting infected. We ran this possibility through our brains. The only clinical reflection that came out was that a lad from Neil's primary school had to go to hospital once for gulping a load down. We reasoned that this might have been because it was antiseptic. We poured Listerine all over Paul's feet and toes.

Our medical team then decided on responsibilities. Ruth took on the clinical role of saying 'This is a really bad idea' repeatedly. She was ejected from the front-line medical team and called a wuss until she stopped. Now we needed an anaesthetist. Ideally, we would have been able to use gas and air, but all we had was a wooden spoon so we decided to go for anaesthesia circa the British Navy in 1750. 'They used to cut people's legs off with just rum and a wooden spoon in the gob,' we told Paul. He was starting to look a bit unsure about the whole thing, but the spoon was popped in his mouth and he agreed that Kevin should take on the bear hug role of making sure that he didn't try to run away. (If you ask me, not enough operations today have patients in really tight bear hugs from big guys reeking of rum and kebab.) Finally, and perhaps most importantly, somebody went to source some more booze (mostly for the surgical team).

At one point as I was getting ready it was suggested (I think, seriously) by one of our medical team that we should consider knocking Paul out. It was pointed out by said member of the team that there was a block of two by four out the back and that he was pretty sure he could knock Paul out with a few shots to the head. One, if he was allowed a chin shot. He was thanked for his contribution and moved on to catering duties for the operation team.

And so it began. Gently at first and then with more gusto as it became obvious that this toenail was going to be playing hardball. The wooden spoon was taking a bit of a pounding from Paul's teeth as I yanked away with all my might. It was clear we were going to need more power. Neil grabbed hold of my waist while I grabbed hold of the toenail with the pliers. This probably didn't look especially medical to any potential observers, but we needed more grunt. Anyway, still no luck. All the while I pulled and pulled and pulled, but the little bastard wasn't budging. I think I may have been getting a little carried away because I announced that I could really do with a scalpel to cut it away from the base a bit more. This provoked a shriek from the hole between the wooden spoon and Paul's teeth, which I took to be non-consent to this subsidiary procedure.

Just at this point the operation had to be stopped because I needed a piss and, just like in any good hospital, when I came back from the toilet I found the patient continuing the operation himself. He wasn't doing badly to be honest. By this point there was a lot of blood around and so I shouted 'suction' because I'd learned from Casualty that this is what you do when you see lots of blood around. I'm not really sure who this was directed to as we had no suction equipment. Neil was confused too because he worriedly replied, 'Suck who?' As head of the medical team I reassured Neil that while the operation was indeed complex, and we were using a number of medical innovations, it didn't necessitate him giving anyone a blow job.

After a lot of pulling it was suggested by

Neil that his toe was getting longer. The patient's that is, not Neil's. As was sensible for any well-trained medical team at this point there was a collective flurry of abuse aimed in Neil's direction. However, he was insistent so we took the unconventional step of breaking off mid-operation to check that the injured toe was the same size as the big toe on the other foot. After this was confirmed there was a further flurry of abuse in Neil's direction, at which point he graphically tendered his resignation from the medical team.

At this point people were beginning to get a little squeamish. There was still plenty of blood but to counter this we reminded ourselves that back in the Navy in the eighteenth century these kinds of operations were standard practice on far worse wounds. Someone raised a dissenting voice to point out that loads of people died for this very reason. In the end we all took turns and it came to look a little bit like a kind of DIY medical Excalibur to see who could pull the sword from the stone. I'm pretty sure that during conventional operations medical staff don't say 'Let me have a go — you're obviously a fucking pussy!' and 'Give it some fucking welly!' In the end the team lost all finesse and the situation turned into one of those fairground punchballs with everyone taking a run up and a whack.

Alas, the toenail still didn't detach. Paul went to a perplexed doctor a few days later who, upon inspection of the pedi-warzone left behind by our ad hoc surgery, asked what exactly had happened. This doctor was apparently not at all impressed with our efforts and Paul was prescribed a course of antibiotics (not Listerine) for the infection and booked for an operation on his toe.

Things wot I learned when I tried to be a doctor . . .

1. There are some things for which a DIY attitude is not only recommended but celebrated. These include changing lightbulbs, replacing bathroom tiles and painting the wall. Removing body parts isn't one of them.
2. Have a plan B. Plan A was to pull the toenail out. When this didn't work, we all just went to bed. This isn't a great plan B for the beleaguered patient.
3. Don't tell the owner of the mouthwash (who was absent) that it was used to treat a festering toenail — they might get funny about it.
4. Don't perform a minor operation when

you can barely see the organ that you are operating on (even though it's quite big) and are feeling a bit sick because of those last few Jäegermeisters.

5. Don't privatize the NHS. Otherwise, like with America, there will be more people performing horrifically (and potentially fatal) inept operations on themselves and their loved ones because they can't afford health coverage.

Length of wait

After making his official request Paul had very little time to wait indeed. We just needed to get home, wait for one of the operating team to throw up, and find some kit. All in all, a couple of hours. Sterling service really, for a complex operation.

Gregory House index (diagnostic capacity)

This is a tough one to ascertain since the diagnosis had actually been made by the patient, who then assembled a medical team to carry out the operation. Hard to tell whether the nail did originally need to come out, or whether it was only after blitzing the whole lower foot area that this became necessary (to remedy the damage we'd caused).

Successful outcome?
If your definition of 'successful' is taking a very minor toenail ailment and making it look like open heart surgery, then, yes, I think it was pretty successful.

Sympathetic and professional health care?
Other than the experiment to see whether his toe had grown, or the one to see if he could still walk without a toe, or the conversation about tonsils and arteries and the use of Listerine as an antiseptic and the fact that nobody could stand up, you couldn't really fault us.

Any signs of inefficiency and poor standards?
One or two.

Front page heading you actually might find in the *Daily Mail*
'Complex operation unsuccessfully carried out by inebriated feral youths using Listerine and pliers.'

An amazing diagnosis

We very rarely find ourselves in positions where we encounter pieces of medical diagnosis that are stunning in their level of educated intuition, mainly because most of the things that we see the doctor for are pretty mundane (e.g. sore throats), or require further tests to confirm (e.g. cancer), or because, through exposure to the internet, the patient may have some idea in advance of what the diagnosis could be. But on one occasion a few years ago I had one of these encounters.

I had had a perpetual pain in my side for a few weeks. Like every self-respecting hypochondriac I have accumulated a diagnostic list of potentially horrendous illnesses that are so brutal in severity that I need to eliminate them from my thinking whenever I start to experience some form of pain or illness. In this case the pain was to the right-hand side of my stomach, not terribly debilitating but persistent nonetheless. So for peace of mind I worked my way through my list:

1. Multiple sclerosis — no tingles, pins and needles, involuntary movements or cognitive failures (unless you count going through a list of highly unlikely diseases a cognitive failure). Ticked off.

2. Parkinson's — no tremor or rigidity of limb movement. As anyone reading this book will know, slow cognitive speed is

an issue but one that has haunted me from birth. Eliminated.

3. Huntington's — for those who don't know, this is a neurodegenerative genetic disorder affecting muscle coordination, resulting in cognitive and psychiatric decline, jerky body movements and an unsteady gait. There is no cure and sufferers end up needing full-time care. In the unlikely event that the diseases we get are selected for us by a giant god in the sky spinning a wheel, I really don't want the counter to stop on this one. Anyway, my mild stomach complaint didn't seem to match the Huntington's symptoms so I moved on.

4. Guinea worm disease — the painful burning sensation as the worm makes its way down to the feet, together with nausea, vomiting and fever means it is often known as 'the fiery serpent'. A quick check of my feet, together with the knowledge that I don't generally drink contaminated water, meant that in this instance I could rule out the fiery serpent (but not before I'd scarred myself for life by googling pictures of its unfortunate victims).

5. Trimethylaminuria (fish odour syndrome) — I asked my wife if I smelt of

fish. She said no so I ticked this one off the list. The wonders of modern diagnostic testing.

6. Cancrum oris (gangrene of the face) — symptoms self-explanatory. If this one isn't on your hypochondria checklist, then you're simply an amateur.

7. Necrotizing fasciitis (flesh-eating bacteria) — seriously, just read the name of it again. Flesh. Eating. Bacteria. Apparently, however, 'flesh-eating' is a misnomer because these bacteria actually operate by destroying the skin and muscles through the emission of toxins — but seriously, who cares? If it looks like your skin is being eaten, your skin is being eaten. End of story. Anyway a quick check revealed that, other than a bit of red skin on my knee, it didn't look like I was being eaten alive. I put the knee on an intensive watch for forty-eight hours before I could eliminate this one. It might be that the bacteria had decided to start in my stomach. I mean, if I was going to eat me then I'd start with the stomach first too.

8. Bubonic plague — any illness nicknamed the 'black death' needs to be on your checklist. You don't just get given titles like that, you have to earn them. People don't go around calling the common cold

the 'congestion death' or hayfever the 'sinussy death'. Its capacity to wipe out a third of the human population (granted, in 1347) means that you don't mess around with it. Anyway, I checked for buboes and acral gangrene (gangrene of the extremities) and it looked like this one could be ruled out too.

9. Rabies — well, I'm not a dog and it's unlikely that I ever will be so, as per usual, I can tick this one off the list. (Its symptoms are so brutal that I can't cross it off permanently. I have to check each time that I'm still not a dog. Just in case.)

10. Fetal familial insomnia — this is where people get to middle age and stop being able to sleep. At all. They then have panic attacks, hallucinations, rapid weight loss, dementia, constipation and pinpoint pupils. I don't know what pinpoint pupils are but it doesn't sound good nestled in amongst that lot. Most people are dead within seven to thirty-six months. A quick check of the pupils revealed that they looked normal. That and I was sleeping OK. Phew.

11. Nodding disease — this involves nodding seizures, and is often triggered by the presentation of food. I often nod when I see food coming my way so this one

needed further investigation. OK, it affects only children, but it is characterized by stunted growth. As I'm only 5 ft 8 in I could actually have been affected by this; for all I know I was meant to be 6 ft 5 in. So I asked my brother if I'd been nodding a lot recently. He told me to stop being a cock. I took this as clarification that I didn't have nodding disease.

12. Ebola (profuse haemorrhaging) — good lord this is a savage disease. It's characterized by profuse haemorrhaging from puncture sites. It just so happened that I had obtained a pretty nasty paper cut earlier that day and close inspection revealed that it wasn't haemorrhaging profusely. I thought I might just be out of the woods for Ebola.

13. Creutzfeldt-Jacob disease — the human version of mad cow disease, associated with progressive dementia, involuntary movements, memory loss and speech impairments before leading to a distressing and painful death. Thank God the stomach isn't mentioned in that list. Looks like I might have escaped CJD again.

14. Genital warts — I know that it might seem odd to tack genital warts onto a list

including MS and Huntington's, but I've seen the pictures on the internet. I defy anyone to see those pictures and think that this shouldn't be on this list. Either way, a quick look down below confirmed that this was unlikely to be the source of my pain.

OK, phew, it looked like I had made it through the maze. I could eliminate this new symptom from my staple go-to illnesses. Time to get to the doctor's.

As I sat in the waiting room I went through my usual process of planning how I was going to present my malady to the doctor so that they didn't think I was a hypochondriac. I was interrupted by an old man with what can only be described as massive ears. And I wasn't the only one who had noticed. There was a lad in there of about five who was also utterly transfixed by these things. I could see he was thinking of saying something, but was trying to figure out whether it was rude or not.

And then he did it. He asked the question that had been on all of our minds. He asked his mum why the man's ears were so big. Ironically, the old man didn't seem to hear it, but the others did and the lad received a telling off for being so rude. That said, even the mum did a double-take when she saw what had prompted her son's inquisitiveness.

As I went into the doctor's office I found that I was still troubled by the whole ears thing. And here was the perfect opportunity to ask a man of medicine. So I did. Dr Holmes looked at my ears to check their size and, upon confirmation that they were far from exceptional, let out a tired sigh when he realized that this question had nothing whatsoever to do with my consultation.

'Is that why you've come today?'

'Er, no. There was a man in the waiting room with huge ears so I just wondered.'

This sounded far sillier after it came out my mouth than it did when it was sitting in the queue of other ridiculous possibilities. To his credit he did answer and confirmed that ears grow as people get older and that some people even think that they are associated with survival. That is, the people who make it to old age are those with big ears. I then felt my ears to see where I stood on this evolutionary divide.

'It's not looking good for you, Carl,' he confirmed whilst trying to suppress a smile. He anticipated me checking his ears and said, 'Oh, don't worry about me; I'll be around for a while.' And he was right. They were by no means a small set of lugs. All of a sudden, I reflected that this consultation had not started exactly as I had wanted.

Now, according to disease specialist John Mann from Johns Hopkins Hospital in Baltimore, the key to a successful diagnosis is doctor-patient chemistry. You should feel comfortable conversing with your doctor, and vice versa. Well, since this doctor only a few months ago was cupping my balls in his hand, I think we'd reached a level of intimacy where we could say that we were comfortable with each other. Even though he probably sees twenty patients a day I suspect he remembers the ones whose balls he has to hold. (I could have been imagining it but I detected a palpable display of relief when I told him that it wasn't my balls in question today.)

Anyway, I always liked Dr Holmes — and not just because he'd been remarkably gentle with my balls, despite having hands that could strangle a blue whale. I also liked him because he was a little bit old school. Crumpled shirt, no-nonsense and, best of all, considerably overweight. This means that unlike some of the other younger, fitter GPs he didn't really care much for those Body Mass Index charts. And this was a good thing for me since I've never looked like the kind of guy who would turn down a Kit Kat. Anyway,

I told him about my stomach pain and I also told him about my own personal diagnoses. That's right — I rocked up with a diagnosis. I'd looked on the internet and thought my symptoms seemed to tally with some sort of problem with my appendix. On one well-known site, I saw the following definition:

Appendicitis is a condition characterized by inflammation of the appendix. It is classified as a medical emergency and many cases require removal of the inflamed appendix, either by laparotomy or laparoscopy. Untreated, mortality is high, mainly because of the risk of rupture leading to infection and inflammation of the intestinal lining (peritoneum) and eventual sepsis, clinically known as peritonitis, which can lead to circulatory shock. Reginald Fitz first described acute and chronic appendicitis in 1886, and it has been recognized as one of the most common causes of severe acute abdominal pain worldwide. A correctly diagnosed non-acute form of appendicitis is known as 'rumbling appendicitis'.

And there we had it. 'Rumbling appendix.' That was my diagnosis.

'I think I might have a rumbling appendix,' I said, with some confidence.

'I see. What makes you come to this conclusion?'

Shit. I hadn't been prepared for that question. I mean, I had just assumed that he'd agree. I was on dangerous ground now.

'It seems to fit all the symptoms.'

'I see. And what are those?'

Well, that question was always coming and to be honest I hadn't adequately prepared for it.

'It's sore and it's around the stomach area . . . And it rumbles.'

'Hmmm, let me do an examination.'

He asked me to lift my shirt. I sucked my belly in as best I could and then lifted. He proceeded to do an examination of the area with his fingers, gently pressing and inquiring as to whether it hurt or not.

'Could you untense your stomach?' Shit, he saw through my best 'pretend you're not a fat shit' trick.

'It is untensed,' I lied. He looked at me suspiciously and this was clearly my signal to let it all flop out. He then asked me if I still cycled a lot. I answered, rather indignantly (since it was clear that my belly had prompted this question about exercise) that indeed I did actually still cycle a lot. Bearing in mind that he was about twice the size of me, I thought it a little cheeky of him to be making a comment about *my* exercise regime so I shot back, 'Do you get a chance to do much exercise yourself?' I thought that should shut any more questions up.

He ignored this question and asked whether I'd got a new bike in the last few weeks. 'No,' I answered in a 'what has that got to do with anything?' tone.

'Hmm, are you sure?'

'Er, yes.' And then it struck me that I had. I had got a new mountain bike a month ago.

'Right, well, I think that's it. Your saddle is too high. You need to lower it an inch or so.' I processed this sceptically. He went on to explain that my rumbling appendix was a very particular type of muscle strain associated with the kind of stretching motion that happens on a bike. 'If you lower the saddle it will be gone in a week or so.'

And sure enough, that is exactly what happened. I would never have guessed this as it didn't seem to particularly hurt on the bike. This was a really sharp piece of diagnosis. A few weeks later my daughter was having some jabs and I bumped into Dr Holmes and confirmed that he had been right. I asked him how he could possibly have known. He told me that he had seen around 250,000 patients pass through his surgery over the years and what single patients probably think of as unique and unusual injuries keep coming back again and again. He said that remembering that I cycled meant it was really a straightforward diagnosis. And with that he was off to see another patient.

Length of wait
Twenty minutes.

Gregory House index (diagnostic capacity)
A diagnosis that would do the man himself proud and an example of why face-to-face, local patient care is so important.

Successful outcome?
Definitely.

Sympathetic and professional health care?
Excellent. He even managed to ignore the juvenile 'I'm not the only one in here who's fat' jibe.

Any signs of inefficiency and poor standards?
Nah, he was great.

Front page heading you won't find in the *Daily Mail*
'Experienced doctor uses his expertise (and

sharp memory) to diagnose muscle strain.'

Dr W and the Dictaphone

One of the things that I have learned over years of interacting with doctors and nurses in the NHS is that, generally, the way they look doesn't impact on how good they are at their job. For instance, in a recent appointment at my local surgery I was assigned to a doctor who wears a range of unusually patterned bow ties (not all at once I might add). Now to my mind bow ties are, in essence, the attire of a clown, not a respected medical professional. When it comes to the person holding the scalpel (or my balls) I don't want 'zany' characters who need to send statements out to the world via the clothes that they wear. I want a higher being from whom all the human traits of neediness, insecurity, fallibility and a desire to be noticed are reassuringly absent. I don't want them to be worn around doctors' necks like a badge. And I'm clearly not alone because whenever I call for an appointment, guess who always has slots free?

But the thing is, I was wrong to avoid him. Because, despite the tie that looked as if it would squirt you with water while its owner cackled into an imaginary camera, when I was finally forced to encounter him when all other doctors were booked up he turned out not only to have an excellent patient manner, but also to be a really good doctor. And he was a thoroughly engaging man to boot. I wanted to tell him that he was a good doctor and that the only thing getting in the way of people seeing this was his looking like he was in training to take over from a retiring Pee-wee Herman.

This GP brings me to the principal protagonist of this section. Dr W, as I shall refer to him from here on in, was a doctor working in south-east London. He was German and he had one very unusual feature; one so idiosyncratic that I have yet to see it in a single other medical professional in thirty-eight years of using them. I am given to understand that, following consultation, doctors — both GPs and consultants — frequently record into their Dictaphones an outline of the consultation so that it can be typed up and added to patient records (or, indeed, form the basis of a communication to the patient or other medical professionals). Dr W was a little different because he cut out the middle man and spoke directly into his Dictaphone while having the consultation. So, in effect, it was a three-way meeting, which is odder than you might imagine; a bit like a conversation on a long-distance telephone line marred by an echo of one of the speakers' voices a second after they speak.

Anyway I went along because I had been having blackouts. I explained this to Dr W, who then pulled out his Dictaphone and started speaking into it. 'Hmm,' I thought, 'That's a little unusual.' He narrated his opener into this machine as 'Mr Walker presents with a headache'. Well, of course, that wasn't exactly what I was saying, and I found myself being drawn into making sure his recording was correct. So I corrected him. As the consultation wore on it was obvious that he held himself to rigorous recording standards and repeatedly said, 'Scrub that' to indicate to whoever had to make sense of these recorded notes that he was starting again. Anyway, to give the reader a flavour I shall give a rough account of how this conversation went.

Dr W: 'What appears to be the issue, Mr Walker?'

Me: 'Well, I've been having some blackouts, episodes where I kind of lose consciousness almost, and my head feels sore . . . '

Dr W (into Dictaphone): 'Mr Walker

presents with a headache.'

Me: 'Well, it's not really a headache; more of a kind of seizure.'

Dr W (into Dictaphone): 'Scrub that; it is not a headache.'

Dr W: 'And for how long have you been experiencing this?'

Me: 'Ooooh, I'd say a few years but it's only recently started to get worse; with greater frequency and intensity, too.'

Dr W (into Dictaphone): 'It has happened for a few years but is getting worse. No scrub that, it is getting more intense.'

Me: ' . . . and more frequent.'

Dr W (into Dictaphone): ' . . . and more frequent.'

Dr W: 'Tell me, Mr Walker, are you overweight?'

Me (lying and simultaneously sucking my belly in): 'I don't know.'

Dr W: 'I think you are.'

Me: 'Oh.'

Dr W (into Dictaphone): 'Mr Walker is probably overweight.' **(Looks away from Dictaphone.)** 'What is your weight?'

Me: 'Er, about thirteen stone.' (I'm obviously taking a stone off to lessen the impending 'don't be a fatty' lecture.)

Dr W (into Dictaphone): 'Mr Walker is a 25-year-old male' **(looks me up and down)** 'of heavy build.'

Me: 'Well, it's actually my head that's quite heavy; I've got a big head.'

Dr W (turns Dictaphone off): 'The body mass index does not take heavy heads into consideration.'

Me: 'Oh.'

Dr W (into Dictaphone): 'Mr Walker is thirteen stone. No, scrub that.' **(He now thinks about a better way of conveying that he doesn't believe I am thirteen stone while looking at my belly to try to determine how big it looks to him.)** 'Mr Walker is over thirteen stone.' **(He looks much more satisfied with this.)**

Dr W: 'Do you have any history of epilepsy in the family?'

Me: 'I don't think so but then I don't know one side of my family very well so it may be that there is.'

Dr W (into Dictaphone): 'Mr Walker may have a family history of epilepsy.' **(He clicks off the recorder and then thinks. He clicks on the**

recorder again.) 'But then he may not.'

And so this went on for the remainder of the consultation. As we went through this process it struck me that there were certain things that probably shouldn't happen in front of you. Things that you knew went on and that you knew had to go on but that people would probably be better off not experiencing with their own eyes. I would put seeing your doctor do his consultation notes in front of you on a pretty exclusive list alongside seeing your parents have sex, seeing your own face as you orgasm and watching your driving-test examiner score your faults as you go through the test. It's just better for everyone if you don't see these.

. Dr W then asked when it was that I had these blackouts and I told him that most commonly they happened after exercise. Now I thought this would open up a line of diagnostic inquiry that might help him to get to the bottom of the blackouts. Instead, he looked startled at the revelation that I exercised. So much so that he found himself asking me again as if he'd misheard me. Now I'm the first to admit that I have a healthy pair of moobs, but this guy was acting as if they'd had to get a crane to lift me through the surgery window for my appointment. His response to my confirmation that I exercised was one of surprise and suspicion. He lifted his Dictaphone to his mouth. He looked like he wanted to share his suspicions with his electronic friend, but he thought better of it.

From this point onward I decided to stick wherever possible to hand gestures rather than replying verbally, principally to amuse myself but also to punish him for looking at me as if someone had stuck Johnny Vegas and John Candy together with Blu-Tack and plonked the composite in front of him. This meant that he couldn't immediately translate my answers into his Dictaphone, which sent him into the kind of raw panic more usually reserved for finding out that someone has sewn up your arsehole when you weren't looking. Anyway, he asked me to verbalize responses rather than just giving him a thumbs up or a shake of my head.

So I started speaking again. I told him that I thought I should come to get checked out as I had read about my symptoms in a book. Dr W, misunderstanding this, then told his Dictaphone that I 'had read a book'. Disappointingly, this also seemed to surprise him. I told him that I wasn't trying generally to steer the conversation onto my literary habits, but that it was a particular book that was relevant to the diagnosis. Once again the Dictaphone was told to 'scrub that'.

Toward the end of the consultation he looked out of the window for what felt like an eternity and gave his Dictaphone a little stroke. It felt like a bit of a private moment between him and his beloved sidekick, but then finally, after a while, he arrived at his conclusion. He told me that he thought I had temporal lobe epilepsy and that I'd need an MRI and an EEG. I asked him what the condition was and what those acronyms stood for. Obviously he then turned on his Dictaphone and told it that I'd asked what the condition was and what the acronyms stood for. He then told me (and the Dictaphone). And there ended the consultation.

I suppose one could get fixated on his mammoth lack of social skills and/or the rather odd use of technology, which savagely ruptured the consultation at regular intervals if one were so inclined. However, I prefer to focus on his diagnostic capability. Within twenty minutes of arrival, and following a number of unnecessary reflections on my weight, I was, for no money, correctly diagnosed with a serious condition and referred on for help. That struck me as pretty special. Scrub that. It *was* special.

Length of wait

Time spent in the waiting room couldn't have been more than twenty minutes. That said, I probably waited a combined total of seventy-two hours while he repeated things into his Dictaphone.

Gregory House index (diagnostic capacity)

Spot on. Despite being a profoundly unusual man, with a curious and disturbing penchant for repeating everything into his Dictaphone, he was bang on the money. He knew what I had even before I had gone for the tests, which meant that a potentially debilitating condition was managed properly. Oddball or not, I am deeply indebted to him for that. I wouldn't tell him that though as he would probably tell his Dictaphone that I was deeply indebted and suggest I spend less money on food.

Successful outcome?

The process was trying but the outcome was excellent.

Sympathetic and professional health care?

Hmmm. This is a tough one. It certainly wasn't unsympathetic or unprofessional; just a very odd kind of professionalism. It was a bit like going to a little Martian doctor, in a little Martian consultation room, on Mars.

Any signs of inefficiency and poor standards?

In a word, no. Inefficiency is defined as a system that does not operate correctly. I went to get help and received the help I needed. Human beings aren't robots. In any public institution of 109,000 doctors there will be a range of different people with different foibles, habits and practices but this is not necessarily the same thing as poor standards.

Front page heading you won't find in the *Daily Mail*

'Doctors, even the odd ones that nobody wants to see, can still sort you out.'

The very best-case scenario

A few years ago I found myself in one of those situations where an NHS worker goes a little bit further than they have to in order to help you out. And it was all due to my impending wedding. After a brief sixteen-year courtship, my partner and I had decided to take the plunge and get married. So, in the run up to the big day, we started to plan the essentials for the wedding:

Organize flowers
Organize a photographer
Sort out transport to and from the reception
Organize a venue
Send out invitations
Organize suits and dresses
Find a way for me not to get hit by a car

Yes, that last one probably does stand out a bit, doesn't it? We agreed that one of the useful things I could do was to stop cycling in the weeks before the wedding. Now I do a lot of cycling; unfortunately, I also do a lot of crashing. Every man has a hobby of some sort. Some like to collect stamps, some like to stuff animals. Me? I like to get knocked off my bike by cars in completely avoidable accidents. So much so that I have my own pair of crutches at home that I stole from Croydon Hospital (sorry, guys).

So far in my battle with car bumpers I am lagging a little bit:

Collision 1   Articulated lorry drives too close to me and one of the metal hooks that secures freight ropes crunches my hand against

the handlebars. Cue blue hand and a lot of swearing at a lorry that has long gone.
Vehicles 1, Carl 0.

Collision 2   Daydreaming, I decide to over-take a car just as the driver of the car decides to turn right. Car runs me over. As I lie on the floor nursing my leg, I don't even have the futile satisfaction of knowing it was someone else's fault.
Vehicles 2, Carl 0.

Collision 3   Car pulls out on me at a junction while I'm travelling at 25 mph. After breaking the windscreen with my head, I find myself lying on the tarmac with a substantial hole in my leg (see page 14). But driver says she didn't see me, so that's all right, then.
Vehicles 3, Carl 0.

Collision 4   The fightback begins. Ish. Car in front of me slams on the brakes and I slam into the back of it. I'm fine, but there is a

massive Carl-shaped dent and scratch in the boot door.
Vehicles 3, Carl 1.

Collision 5   The fightback was brief. On a busy road I decide to get ahead by cycling on the pavement. White van man turns left, obviously not expecting an idiot flying along on the pavement who plants his face into the side of his van. White van man gets out and looks confused. I explain that I'm a bit of a cunt. He seems happy with this explanation.
Vehicles 4, Carl 1.

I also used to race in the local Surrey league and I had had a nasty crash a few weeks earlier. I had been going too fast at a corner on a wet race day, lost the back wheel and took about ten riders down with me. I then did what any self-respecting rider should always do in the moments of confusion that follow a race crash. I got up and shouted, 'Who the fuck did that?' The others followed suit, obviously thinking it couldn't have been me since I kicked off the inquisition. As the mêlée was in full swing, I slunk off home.

After that we thought it would be nice if I managed not to mess up the wedding by being in hospital again. We decided not to take any chances, so I just played a few gentle games of badminton to keep active. What could possibly go wrong?

Duh.

So there I was throwing myself vigorously around the court when, during one game of badminton, I felt my partner kick me quite hard in the calf muscle. So hard in fact that I went down like a ton of bricks. 'What was that for?' I asked, wondering if he'd decided to administer a spot of corporal punishment as a result of my continued failure to get even the softest smash over the net. My plan was to get up and re-negotiate the punishment clause in our team contract when, as I stood up, my leg gave way again and I just as quickly crumpled straight back down to the floor. This wasn't good. I'm not a doctor, but not being able to stand up because one of your legs doesn't work isn't considered a particularly positive state of affairs. My friends had to carry me up to one of their cars for a lift home. As it was five days before the wedding and I'd promised I'd be able to walk down the aisle, I was trying to figure out a gentle way to communicate 'my right leg doesn't work and I don't know why' to what I knew would be a deeply unamused wife-to-be. Sure enough, the sight of me crawling through the front door was about as welcome as a sex video involving our parents. My wife asked me if I was going to be OK for the wedding. I replied with confidence that of course I would. All I had to do was figure out why I couldn't walk.

When it was my turn in A&E I was a little surprised because it appeared that my doctor was the big-toothed one from the Bee Gees (when he was still alive, I might add). I wondered if it was one of those reality programmes like 'Paul Merton does China' or 'Robson Green does extreme fishing'. I looked around for the cameras recording 'Maurice Gibb does *Casualty*', but couldn't find any. After a thorough examination, 'Maurice' revealed (sadly, not in a strained falsetto à la *Tragedy*) that I had a tear on my calf muscle. Now came the key point. I explained to him that I was getting married on Saturday and that I was going to be needing to walk for the big day. So I asked the million dollar question: Did he feel marginalized by the attention that Barry used to get from the girls?

No, not really. It was, of course, 'Will I be able to walk by then?' My wife was in the room with me and, I won't lie, there was a bit of anxiety. I had positioned myself in front of my wife and I was frantically motioning to him that his answer should be 'yes'. The problem was that the tools I had to do this with were quite limited. (I motioned with my eyes for him to say 'yes' and mouthed the word repeatedly.) He looked at me confusedly before suddenly having a eureka moment that I was asking him to say 'yes,' no matter what the actual answer was.

'Oh, yes,' he said, 'you'll be fine. As long as you completely rest it. You might have a slight limp but you'll be fine.'

Nice work, doctor; nice work, indeed. As we were leaving and my wife had gone ahead to get the crutches, I asked him if that was true. He looked at me and with a half-smile told me that that was the *very best* case scenario. I thanked him and hobbled off into the night.

Length of wait
Two hours in casualty.

Gregory House index (diagnostic capacity)
So straightforward was my problem that the doctor said he had already diagnosed it as he saw me walking toward the consultancy room. Apparently, he got people with torn

calves in all the time, although normally through playing squash. I told him that I played badminton like other people played squash. It was meant as an acknowledgement of my limitations but, unfortunately somewhere between my brain and my mouth, the apparatus that put the sentence together ejected the phrase with the tone of an adolescent boast, albeit one that was about as impressive as 'My dad could beat up your dad'.

Successful outcome?
Yes. I went in to find out what was wrong and to be reassured that whatever was wrong would be fine by the wedding day. That pretty much happened as I walked down the aisle with only the glimmer of a limp.

Sympathetic and professional health care?
Very nice. He diagnosed me well, instructed me on what turned out to be a helpful regime of rest and exercises and he even managed not to pay any attention to my badminton boast. Of course, he also did me the favour of a particularly optimistic prognosis.

Any signs of inefficiency and poor standards?
Only by me in the initial choice of sporting

pursuit. The doctor informed me that cyclists tend to have particularly tight leg muscles that are prone to tears through games that involve sudden, quick movements. So if you are a cyclist with a poor concentration span who doesn't want to screw up your wedding day, take up crown bowls for your sporting fix in the run-up to the big day.

Front page heading you won't find in the *Daily Mail*
'Doctor helps man with sore leg.' Definitely *not* front page material.

The female testicologist

OK, so here comes yet another groin examination. The cyst mentioned earlier had grown, not to the point that it could take over New York in a horror film but it was beginning to get uncomfortable while cycling. My appointment with the doctor to deal with it started inauspiciously when the urine sample that I was required to bring started to leak in my bag. I handed over a wet pot to an understanding nurse, who reassured me that I shouldn't worry and that this happens all the time.

I was then called in for the examination

after a fifteen-minute wait spent mainly trying to avoid an old bully I used to know from school in the waiting room. I don't imagine that he's still bullying people at the age of thirty-seven, but just in case he fancied dishing out a Chinese burn or two to keep himself amused, I kept a low profile. As I was called in I was met by a very attractive young doctor who was probably in her early thirties. I had a sudden sinking feeling in the pit of my stomach. The only way that a testicle examination could possibly get worse was if it were carried out by a woman. A pretty woman. I told myself to keep calm, that she was just there to do the paperwork and would soon be replaced by a suitably embarrassed and grizzled old ball doctor. Of course, deep down, I knew differently. A quick chat was terminated with the dreaded words 'Well, let's take a look then'. Everything about my face screamed, 'But you're a woman!!!' I suspect that I looked as disappointed as if she had said, 'OK, let's chop the whole thing off then.' She then brought in another female colleague as some form of chaperone. This new addition was a much older, larger woman whose face suggested that she would throw me out of the window if I even thought about getting an erection. She looked as if she liked to spend her downtime arm-wrestling soldiers in warzones, so I suspect she probably could have done just that. Now I may be unusual here, but I have very little experience of having attractive strangers rummaging around downstairs, so my primary concern now was not showing any visible signs of enjoyment. I had tried to get away with not completely stripping (I thought this might be a good start) and popped the offending ball out of the bottom of my boxers as if it was trying to make a break from its partner. She told me that this wasn't going to cut it and that I'd need to strip.

'How do you feel about having a woman do the examination, Mr Walker?'

'Yeah, fine, no problem.' (*Bloody awful and I'm worried about getting an erection, actually.*)

'I'm going to bring a female colleague to join me; it's just standard procedure with male patients, is that OK?'

'Yeah, of course.' (*Sure, fill your boots. Why don't you go and get a few more, we can sell tickets!*)

'OK, which testicle is it?'

'This one'. (*The one that I'm holding and pushing in your direction. I'm not just showing you this one because I'm particularly proud of it.*)

I needed to find some kind of mental distraction, and fast. I had to make sure that there was no possible way on earth that I would get a semi. After all, I couldn't be sure how I was going to react to an attractive lady with her hands on my testicles. And then suddenly I was rescued by Jan Michael Vincent, or 'Airwolf' as he was better known. I have no idea why Airwolf popped into my head at the critical moment but I wasn't too displeased. I started thinking about whether I would prefer to be rescued by Airwolf or Knight Rider. I nodded politely to the arm-wrestling chaperone to reassure her that I was behaving myself. She continued to look at me like I was a professional sex pest on a busman's holiday.

As my testicles were being kneaded I reflected that most of the situations where I might require rescuing would probably happen in an area that would be difficult to park a helicopter in, and so, purely from a practical perspective, it would make more sense to call on Michael Knight. Of course, the fact that Michael Knight spent his later career hiding his man boobs while running along the beach on *Baywatch* kind of soiled his appeal. At this point I noticed that I was paying no attention to what the doctor was saying. Since she might be talking about cancer or operations or something I figured that I should tune back in. The threat of an erection incident had been neutralized.

I pulled my trousers back up and we sat at her desk. She explained that the cyst had grown, but that it was not particularly big; that she had in fact seen bigger. I wasn't sure if she was still talking about the cyst here but gave her the benefit of the doubt. She explained that although it may irritate at times, having it removed could be a very painful and difficult operation. More importantly, there could be a lot of bleeding involved. She then asked me whether that was something that I would want. Now I can't speak for others here but I've never been a great fan of massive testicular bleeding and told her so. We agreed then that the cyst was better left where it was. As I walked out of the consultation room it struck me that this was a clearly intelligent woman, who would have studied and worked hard for many, many years and her reward was to hold my plums while I thought about Airwolf. Truly, being a doctor is a vocation.

Length of wait
About twenty minutes, five of which were spent apologizing for handing over a bottle covered in piss.

Gregory House index (diagnostic capacity)
So far, so good.

Successful outcome?
Mixed. I came in to get told that no one was going to go near my balls with a scalpel, and that my cyst could be removed by non-invasive treatment (something like a magic wand). Following a sensitive, brief and painless examination, I went away having met the first objective. However, I was also told I'd have to live with the cyst. That was less ideal.

Sympathetic and professional health care?
Given that I covered one woman's hands in piss and made another one hold my balls, my treatment was very considerate and professional.

Any signs of inefficiency and poor standards?
The small plastic tubes they distribute for you to collect your urine in could possibly be a little more robust, but other than that the standards were excellent. We even had our own bodyguard to launch me out of the window if I even thought about getting a boner.

Front page heading you won't find in the *Daily Mail*

'Doctor tells man his balls are OK.' Never going to shift newspapers, that one.

Forrest Gump visits Worthing

A few years ago I found myself entering my local general practice for some kind of allergic reaction that I had had to something or other that had allowed hives to run all over my body like hundreds of tiny climbers trying to ascend a particularly fat mountain. As I entered the practice I noted that they had introduced a machine that patients use to sign in on arrival. It was a very simple piece of equipment where you had to type in your gender and date of birth. That was literally it. The gender bit I seemed to manage without much problem, after all there was a 'male' touch box and a 'female' touch box.

However, when we moved to 'date of birth' it all got a bit tricky. I managed the month I was born but, to be fair, you'd probably expect that of a man in his late thirties. But then it asked me to type the day number. It provided touch boxes for the numbers one to thirty-one. I was born on 23 June, but for some reason instead of pressing '23' I kept typing the '2' and then the '3'. And, of course, it wouldn't work. This is because the machine wasn't designed to cater for goons.

I then started trying to press the '2' and '3' really quickly as if by speed of hand I could iron out the clear failing of this piece of medical technology and trick it into letting me register. The lady at reception saw me employing my 'quick hands' brainwave and took it upon herself to point out that just pressing '23' would probably do the trick. Feeling like an utter plum I thanked her and then went and sat down and hid in the corner of the waiting room.

The disappointment of watching successive patients come in and use the system with ease was interrupted by an announcement that the doctor was running ten minutes late. I decided to take this opportunity to nip to the loo. This was where an already mildly embarrassing morning took a turn for the worse. After washing my hands I found that I was in fact not able to leave the toilet. Not because I had grown uncharacteristically attached to it, but because for some reason the lock that locked the door from the inside wasn't moving. For about five minutes I tried everything in my power to pull that lock back, but it would not budge for love nor money. Now I was in a real situation. I needed to consult my box of tricks for what to do if you're stuck in a public toilet. I won't lie, it was pretty bare. I thought about shouting 'help', but that didn't seem quite right. I mean, it's not like I was in any immediate danger. I wasn't trapped in the toilet with a crocodile. I decided that a much better idea was to knock on the door, so I gave a few firm knocks and waited with my ear to the door to hear whether my distress had been picked up by anyone.

It then dawned on me that if I was a patient and I heard somebody knocking from the inside of a toilet, I probably wouldn't go to investigate either. I'd just assume that there was a weirdo in there. So I then called out 'Hello?' followed by an 'Is there anyone there who can hear me?' I was aware that there was a pretty full waiting room so thought that this should do the trick. Still no response. Perhaps I just sounded like I was trying to make conversation. And had I been passing the door, would I have really said 'Hello' back to a disembodied voice in a toilet?

I then tried to push at the door and was straining loudly. I imagine that I must have sounded like a man trying to force a bowling ball out of his arse so I stopped that. Now it says something about my sense of personal vanity that at this point Indiana Jones popped into my head. I guess this was because he was always finding himself trapped in difficult situations, although to be fair I don't remember any of the films featuring him trapped in a toilet that had a stiff door latch. I felt suddenly emboldened by the thought that Indiana Jones would also be flummoxed by my present dilemma. His normal tactic to get out of entrapment was to use his whip to swing from a convenient roof beam or the underside of a fast-moving horse. No beams or horses in here, Indiana. You'd be sat on this bog just like me. This was good, I was already feeling better.

I thought of calling the practice to explain that I was trapped in their toilet. Indeed I tried, but I couldn't get a signal on my phone. I went back to plan B and shouted 'Hello?' loudly again. This time an elderly lady came to the door and announced that there was a lot of noise coming from inside the toilet. The tone of her voice was quite admonishing, as if I was having an excessively loud number two and rudely disturbing the peace of the other waiting patients. Still, she was my lifeline and I needed to treat her with respect. 'I'm trapped,' I announced. 'You're who?' she replied, obviously not hearing me particularly well. I asked her if she could go and get the receptionist, to which she replied that I was making a lot of noise in the toilet. 'So would you if you were trapped in a toilet,' I managed to stop myself from saying. Instead, I asked her to please get a receptionist. But the voice had gone, no response.

I sat down and mulled over worst-case scenarios. Maybe I'd be here all day and then they would all go home and I'd be stuck in here for three days. After all, this was a Friday. Maybe I was going to die in a toilet like Elvis. This thought spurred me back over to the door. I didn't want to go out like that. Then a new voice came along and asked if I was OK. This was a different voice from the old lady, a younger voice not trying to get me to make less noise — I could do business with this voice.

I sheepishly told my new potential rescuer that I couldn't get out because the lock was stuck. 'Do you want me to help?' came the reply. No, not at all, I thought, I just wanted to let someone know, really. Of course I wanted help! Under what circumstances could someone point out that they were trapped in a public toilet and then possibly *not* want help? Still, be cool, I told myself, this new lady was my lifeline. Suddenly the door opened and I found myself moving quickly out through the gap as if I was only going to be given a certain amount of time before I was shut back in again.

It was the same lady who had helped me steer through the simplicities of the electronic registration system. Now the look she wore on her face was a sympathetic one. She looked again into the toilet as if she might find my carer in there too. 'The lock was stuck, probably happens all the time?' I asked more in hope than anything else.

'No, this is the first time.' Now I felt like someone who pretended to get stuck in toilets so that they could be rescued. 'But I'll get someone to look at it, I'm sure it could do with being oiled or something,' she said, unconvincingly. I could see a pretty full waiting room looking at me with a mixture of amusement and confusion. In the vain hope that I could rescue some dignity I replied loudly so that they could all hear, 'Yes, probably just a bit of WD40 needed on that lock.' I might just as well have announced, 'Yes, I'm an utter moron' for all the effect it seemed to have on those who were still visibly trying not to laugh.

Now I had to do the walk of shame, past all of the people who knew that I had got trapped in the toilet. Past disappointed receptionists, disappointed patients, disappointed children and the old woman who gave me a filthy look as if to say, 'So it was you making all that bloody racket in the toilet!' The receptionist was ever so apologetic and to make amends she brought me a cup of tea. Now, not only did I look like someone too dim to open a toilet door, but I also looked so fragile as to need help to cope with the trauma. Really nice of her, though. She said that she'd put an 'out of order' sign on the door immediately. However, we both knew that the 'out of order' sign should probably have been hung on me.

Length of wait
Quite a long time really.

Gregory House index (diagnostic capacity)
Everyone in the waiting room made their own diagnosis.

Successful outcome?
Well, I got out of the toilet. I know it sounds as though my standards have dipped since the book started, but at the time it was touch and go whether I'd even manage that.

Sympathetic and professional health care?
Really nice. They couldn't have been more friendly or supportive. They treated me as a

victim of a breakdown in their infrastructure rather than a man who had been brought up on a farm by a family of dim goats. And that was nice.

Any signs of inefficiency and poor standards?

I went back in to double-check the stiffness of the lock with the receptionist so that I could show her the problem. On all five times that I tried the lock it moved effortlessly. 'I don't understand, it was stuck fast,' I bleated. 'It really was.' She said that she didn't doubt it and that they'd get someone in to fix it. If I were her I'd probably take the 'out of order' sign down the moment I left the practice. You don't need to call out a locksmith at £60 an hour to diagnose a moron.

Front page heading you won't find in the *Daily Mail*

'Man auditions for role in the new Chuckle Brothers film.'

Dry food, stomach linings and other associated medical myths

There are a whole load of medical myths out there that people often draw upon to govern their health behaviour. They are, in essence, absolute bollocks, but that doesn't stop us from passing them on with no little sense of authority. For instance, I have found myself telling people that we actually only use 10% of our brains. Is it true? No chance. Apparently, MRI scans, PET scans and other imaging studies show no dormant areas of the brain, and even viewing individual neurons or cells reveals no inactive areas. It is thought that this particular myth originated with the birth of the self-improvement industry in the 1900s; an industry predicated on convincing people that its bag of tricks could help them to reach their full potential.

I've also found myself telling various people that the more we shave, the thicker the hair grows back. Is it true? Nope, absolute nonsense. A clinical trial compared hair growth in shaved patches to growth in non-shaved patches. The hair which replaced the shaved hair was no darker or thicker, and did not grow any faster. More recent studies have confirmed that one.

And what about sugar making children hyperactive? Surely that's true? We all know what happens when you give children too much sugar — they go mental. Of course they do. Nope, utter shite apparently. Paediatricians at the Riley Hospital for

Children recently said: 'In at least 12 double-blinded, randomized, controlled trials, scientists have examined how children react to diets containing different levels of sugar.' None of these studies, not even studies looking specifically at children with Attention Deficit Hyperactivity Disorder (ADHD), could detect any differences in behaviour between the children who had sugar and those who did not. Apparently, this includes artificial and natural sources of sugar. Interestingly, in the study, parents who were told their children had been given sugar when they hadn't, noted that the child was more hyperactive. So it seems it is all in the parent's mind.

Now I've often amazed myself with some of the things that I have found myself saying about the human body. My process for the dissemination of body facts seems to be that I think something, assume it must be true because there is no one there to tell me it's bollocks and then tell everyone else about it as if it is true.

Carl Walker's top medical 'facts'

1. **Milk irritates the stomach lining** — I have found myself speaking with some authority about this, but in reality I have

no idea whether we even *have* stomach linings and I certainly don't know why milk would bother them if we have. I think this was one passed down from my mum. That this was the same woman who told me that little fairies remove your teeth and replace them with coins that they put under your pillow when you are sleeping doesn't seem to have engendered any scepticism in me.

2. **Human beings don't need noses** — I recall saying this a lot during my younger years after I saw a B-movie where the aliens didn't have noses. It took me a few years to figure out that breathing and eating would be a far trickier multitask without them.

3. **There are no such things as grey hairs** — in my infinite wisdom I have decided that there are only white hairs and that the colour grey comes from the mixture of white and the person's natural colour. My process of verification for this particular fact is not to look closely at anyone with grey hair, but instead just decide that it's probably true. Science of the highest order.

4. **You can get tonsillitis without having tonsils** — my personal favourite.

5. **If there is no space for a wisdom tooth**

to come through, it will eventually push through anyway and fracture your jaw and swell your brain — literally no idea where this one came from, although I have a sneaky feeling it may have emerged from a drunken conversation when I was at university where someone told me that their friend didn't get their wisdom tooth seen to and they ended up with a dislocated face (or something).

6. **Old men's scrotums (or is it scrota?) can be so elastic that when sitting on the loo their balls can touch the water** — obviously I'm quite selective about who I share this particular 'fact' with. When I was a teenager an older guy I worked with once told me that his balls did indeed touch the water so he had to sit on specially made cushions with holes in them to prop him higher above sea level. He told me that this was the case for all old men. I'm not sure it's true but I always like repeating it to people just for the looks on their faces.

7. **Dry food** — finally, the particular topic relevant to this instance of NHS use — how to feed a stomach recovering from a stomach bug. To my mind you always need to stick to dry food in order not to

irritate the stomach lining (which may or may not exist). Dry biscuits, dry toast, anything dry. That's the rule.

So when my little one had picked up a nasty case of stomach flu, we tried to restart her on dry foods to help her keep her strength up. The problem was that every time we gave her anything she threw it back up within thirty minutes. After four days of this it was getting a little bit much so we popped down to our local A&E. When the doctor came along and examined my daughter she told us not to worry. As long as she was drinking water then four days without food was fine. That was the first revelation of this particular visit. If I don't eat for four hours I curl up in a corner and slowly start to die (all the while screaming for my mum). The second revelation came in response to our telling the doctor that once her stomach had settled we were restarting her with light, dry foods. I won't lie, at this point I was expecting a bit of praise from the doctor for doing the right thing. I sat back ready for a well-earned 'well done'. Instead, I was told that this was a very bad idea.

Eh?

So entrenched was this folk belief in my brain that I momentarily lost my bearings and told this doctor, with many years of training and experience, that dry things were better for stomach linings. I said it in my most polite 'not a lot of people know this' voice. She asked why I thought this was the case but the best I could come up with was that dry things weren't wet. That kind of deduction is unlikely to win you an argument anywhere in the world. She replied, more firmly this time, that not only was this not true but that dry things were actually more likely to irritate recovering stomachs. Now some folk beliefs are difficult to shake and even at this point I was wondering how a doctor could have missed such an obvious fact. However, on realizing that the only argument I had left in the locker to support my position was that 'my mum told me so', I knew I was probably on shaky ground. As a child I swore I wouldn't listen to her ever again after the whole Father Christmas debacle, but it seems I hadn't learned.

The doctor's advice was to start slowly with baby pouches, just one spoonful at a time and build up. The key was to make sure the food was soft and wet. She looked at me pointedly when she said the word 'wet'. I looked at the floor. We thanked the doctor, took her advice and Anna didn't throw up again.

Length of wait
A couple of hours in A&E but since my daughter hadn't eaten for four days and was in a dreadful state I felt that this was a pretty worthwhile trade-off if I could see someone who would make her well.

Gregory House index (diagnostic capacity)
She managed to diagnose both a young girl recovering from stomach flu and an adult male hampering that recovery through his ignorance.

Successful outcome?
It's hard to overestimate the impact of someone helping you to get your child to eat again after four days of relentless vomiting. Two hours of waiting, no money and they will take your ill child and make them well. It doesn't get much better than this.

Sympathetic and professional health care?
Very professional. We were triaged and then led to a children's waiting room after which a sympathetic and professional five-minute consultation sorted the problem. She could have responded to my dry food gibberish by saying, 'You have come to seek my expertise

245

so shut up and do what I say,' but she didn't.

Any signs of inefficiency and poor standards?
Not in the slightest.

Front page heading you won't find in the *Daily Mail*
'Doctor's advice immediately stops toddler throwing up after four days.'

Carl Walker vs the world: the ethical conundrum

A recent study investigating patients' perceptions of entitlement to time in general practice consultations for depression in eight general practices in the West Midlands showed that patients had an intense sense of time-pressure and exhibited a kind of self-imposed rationing of time in consultations. Indeed, this anxiety about time affected patients' freedom to talk about their problems. Patients apparently often take it upon themselves to manage time in the consultation in order to relieve the time burden they perceive their doctors to be working under. While the average consultation time may be eight minutes, this is often because that is the time that patients feel entitled to rather than because we have a nation of impatient doctors putting on big boots to kick you out of their practice.

I've actively tested this theory in a number of practices over recent years and overall I have to say that it holds. If you want to take your time they pretty much let you. I have one particular GP who excels in this field. So relaxed and inviting is he that an enquiry into how they were able to identify my salmonella poisoning led to a prolonged explanation that took in the origins of cholera, the work of the great nineteenth-century medical epidemiologist John Snow and a potted history of the way in which the public health system in the UK generally responds to infectious diseases.

Once I visited this GP when my tonsils were taking one of their frequent mid-winter breaks from sitting in the back of my throat like good little tonsils should. I had a particularly bad bout and had been up all night with a fever. As one does in these circumstances I headed straight to my GP the next day to get some antibiotics. What I expected to be a simple three-stage process where he looked at my tonsils, signed a prescription pad and then said goodbye instead ended up with me being presented, rather unusually, with an ethical conundrum.

Indeed, it was a conundrum that required me to think about my needs in relation to the needs of my country. Now I have never been especially strong in such circumstances. The three examples below highlight this:

Conundrum I: do you steal toilet roll from train station toilets?

When living as a poor student in London I stumbled upon a way to cut our household living costs. I realized that toilet roll was an altogether unnecessary purchase since I could go to London Bridge station and steal the ludicrously big rolls of toilet paper that they used in the public toilets. So that's exactly what I did. I shoved them in my bag and disappeared off into the night like a particularly undignified Robin Hood. After all, every penny counted. And it worked too. I would regularly rock up at our shared house as a kind of Santa Claus of lavatory supplies, dishing out toilet rolls to all the kids who'd been good that year.

One day I tried to steal two of the huge rolls. Like all great thieves I had eventually got greedy. Just as Al Capone was brought down by not paying his taxes, I was brought down by a guard who spotted me carrying two massive toilet rolls in a frankly ill-equipped bag. The guard didn't respond well to my pretty ropey on-the-spot excuse that 'I wasn't stealing it; I was just about to go and refill it.' This guy wasn't Poirot but he had sufficient intellectual acuity to ask why someone who wasn't employed at the station would take it upon themselves to start refilling the station's toilet-paper holders. And why was I heading *away* from the toilets? My answer that it was just a hobby didn't seem to cut any ice since his next observation was that they cut thieves' heads off in Saudi Arabia. I actually think it's their hands but quibbling about this seemed a little petty.

Conundrum 2: do you blame a fat person for eating sausage rolls that you ate?

I found myself in a different type of ethical conundrum at an event at work recently. I didn't realize it at the time but I'd pulverized the sausage roll tray at the buffet that they had organized for between presentations. And I mean pulverized. I had really gone to town on this dish. Out of about twenty sausage rolls there were maybe four or five left. And this was before break-time and before anyone had taken the cling film off the rest of the buffet dishes. I decided here that attack was the best defence and so I developed a two-part plan to throw people off the scent. Firstly, I went around to anyone who'd listen, asking them if they saw who ate the sausage rolls and looking let down by the exploits of this imaginary thief. Secondly — and I'm not proud of this — I intimated my suspicion that one of the larger guests might have savaged the plate while we were all in the last presentation. I figured I was on safe ground as nobody would challenge said guest for fear of being accused of being discriminatory. I was now the one person in the room who was off the hook for the sausage roll theft.

Conundrum 3: if you accidentally kill a gerbil do you tell anyone?

This is another one I'm not especially proud of, although in mitigation I was only nine. I was visiting a friend and waiting in his bedroom for him to finish something or other. I noticed his gerbil in the cage in the corner of his room so I entertained myself by having a little play with it. It was running on a wheel but looked like it was getting a little fatigued so I thought I'd give it some help. I think I can probably say it now that he's passed to the other side, but he wasn't a small gerbil. In particular, he was carrying some timber around his backside which I thought he'd benefit from getting rid of. I started to give the wheel a spin. An almighty spin. Sammy tried to keep up at first and made a pretty good fist of it, his lardy gerbil butt pounding the steps of his ferris wheel. In fact, I'd go as far as to say he was enjoying himself as much as me. To this day I believe he flashed me a big gerbil smile of pleasure as he galloped round his wheel.

However, after a while he just collapsed. I gave him a gentle push but nothing. It was becoming obvious to this nine-year-old brain that I had killed my friend's gerbil. *Accidentally*, I need to stress at this juncture. (Nobody wants to be known as a gerbil-killer, no matter what age you are.) I wasn't aware of whether there was any kind of gerbil CPR regime that could be employed to bring Sammy back. Even if there was, is that *really* what Sammy would have wanted? The guilty little boy staring at the supine rodent in his cage decided that Sammy would have wanted a dignified death rather than have a crash team pumping away at him. So I left him alone and said nothing. At all. To anyone. To this day I'm expecting to meet a baseball bat-wielding Sammy in the next world.

So, anyway, you get the picture. I allow myself a degree of latitude when it comes to potential ethical conundrums. Now, on this consultation, my GP took it upon himself to tell me a little bit about antibiotics as he was concerned that I'd had to take three sets in little more than a month for my recurring tonsillitis. He told me that the antibiotic would still be effective for me, but that prolonged use would decrease its effectiveness. Moreover, the more often we use antibiotics, the less likely it is that they will work for other people since it increases the chance of strains of bacteria developing resistance to the antibiotic.

Now this came as news to me. But with this in mind he said that I needed to make the decision regarding whether or not to take this dose dependent on the severity of the pain I was in because I would be speeding up my recovery by a day or two, but making it less likely as a whole for other people. Indeed, he told me about the altogether more draconian system for antibiotics that they have in the Netherlands for this very reason. There, to protect against a weakening of a given antibiotic, you literally have to be at death's door to get your hands on it.

So, with that in mind, he asked if I still

wanted some. Of course, for the gerbil-killing, sausage roll-demolishing, toilet-roll thief inside me this barely even registered. My immediate internal response was, 'Er, yeah,' but I couldn't help thinking that such a quick dismissal of this ethical dilemma would have disappointed my doctor, so I waited a while and pretended that I was considering the pros and cons of the matter. 'It's not easy,' I lied and looked some more as though I was giving it thought. This pleased my GP, who could see that I'd taken on the gravity of the situation. But gerbil murderers who are still at large thirty years after the crime are nothing if not cunning. 'I think this time I'll take them because of the level of pain,' I said solemnly as if the decision hurt me personally and there might be some other time when I wouldn't make this decision (there won't).

So he wrote me the prescription and I thanked him for taking the time and explaining it. While in my case he was always wasting his time since I am an ethical remedial, not everyone would steal large rolls of bog paper that wasn't theirs, so it didn't in any way make this procedure fruitless. What I appreciated was that he took the time to explain it to me, to contextualize my choice and to make me feel as though I wasn't just being pushed through a medical sausage machine.

Length of wait
Around twenty-five minutes.

Gregory House index (diagnostic capacity)
Sadly lacking. My GP treated me as though I were someone with a social conscience.

Successful outcome?
Yup, I got my antibiotics, and society as a whole was just that little bit worse for it.

Sympathetic and professional health care?
Very much so. He was patient, informative and I quite liked being treated as if I wasn't the kind of man who blamed nearby fat people for eating sausage rolls that he had scoffed.

Any signs of inefficiency and poor standards?
Not in the slightest. You could quibble about the twenty-five minute wait, but that just tells me that he is taking his time with other patients. I could be another patient who needs that time one day so I prefer to think of

this as flexibility rather than inefficiency.

Front page heading you won't find in the *Daily Mail*
'GP takes time to explain implications of repeated antibiotic use to a gerbil-killer.'

Dealing with idiots 3: bleeding nipples

Everyone, no matter what age they are, no matter how well-educated they are, has some fundamental gaps in their knowledge of the world. Every person has a knowledge Achilles' heel, something that they should have come to know, that the rest of the world came to know, but that just somehow passed them by. I'll give you an example. And bear in mind as I give this example that I am a reasonably well-qualified, well-educated, professional person. A couple of years ago my wife and I were in the supermarket doing our daily Tuesday evening shop after work. The division of labour during these trips was that my wife did the thinking, choosing of foods and selection of fresh produce, while I grabbed multibags of Hula Hoops and tried to see how far along the aisle I could make it if I treated the trolley as a makeshift skateboard. Obviously, both of our inputs were essential to the shopping process.

We were hovering around the fruit and veg aisle when my eye was caught by a bunch of unusually large lemons. As I approached them my initial impression was confirmed. These were amazing, the biggest lemons I had ever seen. I was understandably keen to share my finding with my wife and said, 'Good God, Ruth, look at the size of these lemons.' I won't lie, I was pretty excited and had already decided that they were the result of some wacky GM exercise by a group of juvenile scientists. It's hard to describe the look my wife gave me other than to say it's probably similar to the look that a vet gives an old sick dog just before he puts it down.

'These are grapefruits,' she said quietly and with a tone of solemn regret, no doubt reflecting back on the moment she agreed to marry me. It turns out that, up until my late twenties, I had always thought that grapefruits looked like pineapples. Other than to say I'm not much of a fruit man, there's no excuse.

Most people have at least one of these knowledge gaps. However, it appears that I have a few, and this second example required that I went to a doctor to receive the enlightenment that my wife so disappointingly supplied in the fruit and veg aisle at

Morrisons. When I was a youngster I used to do a lot of running. After a five-year sabbatical to concentrate on cigarettes and putting on weight, it became obvious to me in my late twenties that it might be a smart idea to take it up again. But two key things had changed in the intervening period. One was on the left-hand side of my chest and the other was on the right-hand side. That's right, moobs. On the way back from my first run I was in the process of congratulating myself when my flatmate pointed out that I looked like I had been shot. I looked down and sure enough my white running T-shirt was covered in blood. Obviously, with blood on a white T-shirt I did what anyone would do and pretended to be a zombie in the bathroom mirror — this is an opportunity that doesn't present itself every day. Having got the serious business out of the way I had to then figure out *why* I was bleeding. Taking my T-shirt off didn't help as my chest had no blood on it whatsoever. Where on earth could the blood have come from? My conclusion? I'm not a particularly dim man (although I know the whole grapefruit thing suggests otherwise) but the only thing I could think of was that I had sweated blood. That's right, I had put in so much effort that I had actually started to *sweat blood*. By

God, I thought, I've pushed myself too far! I must be some kind of marine or something because I sweated blood and I didn't even notice it.

I had thought this notion of sweating blood was just a turn of phrase but my T-shirt was telling me something quite different. (This was an era on the cusp of the internet so I didn't have a ready resource to run it by.) If I was sweating blood I was going to have to do something about it. So, as I sat in the waiting room of my local surgery, it dawned on me that, despite years of thinking myself a wuss, I might actually be quite hard. I thought about other hard people who were likely to go for a jog, sweat blood and not even notice it. The first name that came into my head was John J. Rambo. As I waited for the doctor I started to reflect on whether Rambo would have gone to his GP to get it checked out. Of course, he wouldn't; he would probably have punched his chest until it stopped bleeding. Because that's what Rambo does. This was a man who 'could eat things that would make a billy goat puke'.

Luckily I was drawn out of my ruminations by the doctor calling me in. Now, unlike during Grapefruit-gate, I was aware that if I asked the doctor straight out whether it's possible to sweat blood he might think I was an idiot so I needed a strategy that didn't involve me actually asking that question. What took place is probably best reported verbatim. The conversation went like this:

Doctor: 'So Mr Walker, how can I help you today?'

Me: 'Hi, doctor, just recently I came back from a five-mile run (it was three but that sounds a bit pathetic so I added a couple on) and when I got back there was blood all over the front of my T-shirt.'

Doctor: 'I see, do you jog regularly?'

Me: 'Run, it was a run, not a jog.' (Nobody sweats blood while they jog; I couldn't have him thinking I was jogging. And anyway Rambo would run, not jog.)

Doctor: 'I see.'

Me: And when I got back I noticed that there was blood all over the front of my T-shirt.'

Doctor: 'OK, how much blood?'

Me: 'Er, quite a lot.'

Doctor: 'Would you say as much as a cup?'

Me: 'Oh God, yeah! I mean, it was a lot; more like a dead animal. You know if you see one on the road? — like that.'

Doctor: 'Right, a big dead animal or a small one?'

Me: 'A medium-sized one. Like a fox maybe.' (If I'm honest, the whole dead animal thing wasn't really moving us forward.)

Doctor: 'What part of your chest was it?'

Me: 'It was the top of my chest. I was sweating a lot so maybe that was something to do with it, I was running quite hard. (OK, so here it was, the line that was gently prompting him to answer my sweating blood question without me looking like an absolute dick.)

Doctor: 'Are you asking me if you were sweating blood?'

Me: (Oh shit, that wasn't meant to happen.) 'Oh God, no! Of course not — ha ha.'

(Long pause)

Me: 'Was I?'

Doctor: 'No.'

Me: 'No, no, of course not, I didn't think so.'

Doctor: 'Has this happened any time other than when you jog?'

Me: 'No.'

Doctor:	'Then I suspect what we have here is a classic case of chafed nipples.'
Me:	'Chafed nipples?' (All of a sudden my Rambo pretensions were on pretty rocky ground. I'd gone from sweating blood to bleeding nipples, from Rambo to Ian Beale.)
Doctor:	'Yes.'
Me:	'Is it because I have disco tits? It's OK. You can tell me.'
Doctor:	'Disco what?'
Me:	'Man boobs. Moobs.'
Doctor:	(laughing) 'No, not at all, this is quite a common experience especially in people who don't run much. Your nipples will harden up with time if you keep running, so don't worry about it.'

Now, you would have been hard-pressed to find someone less deserving of the time of a medical practitioner than I was then. Well, maybe apart from my mate Nick who once went to see a doctor in order to get confirmation of whether or not he was going bald. Regardless of this, the doctor didn't give me a withering look and throw me out. Instead, he told me not to worry about my moobs, said that I was doing really well to run and suggested nipple plasters until the skin firmed up. He really gave me a thumbs up for what I was trying to do, and did some serious health promotion work in the process, rather than discouraging me by telling me not to be such a dick. In fact, by the time I left the surgery I had forgotten about the whole chafed nipple/sweating blood thing and was feeling pretty good about myself.

Length of wait
About half an hour.

Gregory House index (diagnostic capacity)
Chafed nipples. Perhaps the most unsatisfying diagnosis I have ever received in my life.

Successful outcome?
No. I found out that I wasn't really like Rambo after all. Rambo fell 100 ft into some trees that ripped open large gashes in his flesh. He sewed these up himself in the wild with makeshift tools. I had slightly chafed nipples and ran crying to my GP.

Sympathetic and professional health care?
I left the surgery reflecting on the fact that I was glad my doctor was nicer than me. I would have laughed for half an hour and then

gone into the waiting room and announced, 'Hey, everyone, you'll never guess what — some dick in here thinks he's sweating blood.' And then laughed for another half an hour.

Any signs of inefficiency and poor standards?
Nope, not in the slightest.

Front page heading you won't find in the *Daily Mail*
'Timewaster with sore nipples isn't immediately kicked out for timewasting by GP.'

Conclusions on a changing National Health Service

Since I started this book with a story about my older brother it seems fitting that I finish it with one. When I was around seven years old I remember that I was sitting at the kitchen table minding my own business when my older brother decided to make a cup of tea. He lifted up the kettle and carried it to his cup, which he had, for some reason known only to himself, placed at the opposite side of the kitchen. As he went to transport the scalding hot water my mum told him to be very careful not to drop it. I can only assume that this sounded to him a bit like 'Throw that full kettle of boiling hot water on your brother's legs,' since this is exactly what happened.

Now at this point my mum, a single mother of three living on a council estate in Kilmarnock, who at the time was on a medical secretary's course at the local technical college, had one single concern on her mind — getting her son to the hospital. She wasn't thinking about whether her health premiums were up-to-date or whether medical attention would end up sending her into the arms of bailiffs. She had the luxury — and make no mistake, it *is* a luxury — of simply focusing on getting me to the hospital.

Looking back on the contents of this book I have drawn the conclusion that my NHS life really has been pretty good. It has been characterized by sympathetic and attentive health care, excellent diagnoses in a whole range of issues from my balls to my brain to my lower back, and the standards throughout my interaction with the service — an interaction that has ranged from central Scotland to central London and taking in Surrey and West Sussex — have been excellent. The illnesses, injuries, sniffles, hypochondrias, rashes and neurological screw-ups that I have experienced through my thirty-eight years have been rich and varied. And like the 92% of hospital patients who are satisfied with their treatment, and the nearly 90% of GP users satisfied with their treatment, my NHS life has been a good one.

It's been a good one because the infrastructure, the people and the ethos of the organization have been, on the whole, outstanding. However, despite this, and despite the field hospitals in the USA that stand as a stark monument to the vagaries of a privatized health care system, there is a small but profoundly influential group of politicians, lobbyists and private health care representatives eager to radically change it. To reinvent a wheel that moves along the ground with consummate ease because at the moment that wheel isn't making *them* any money. And should they be successful, the NHS lives that we take for granted will, for many, cease.

Instead, we will have a system where many people will self-medicate to profoundly detrimental effect. Coverage will be partial and very skewed. Our health needs will be a secondary priority to the satisfying of shareholders eager for profits out of our aches, pains, strains, clots and breaks. And, if we're lucky, a benevolent field hospital might come our way sometime soon before we or a loved one dies of an otherwise preventable illness.

We already know the reasons not to privatize. They have been stated and reiterated throughout this book: the fact that the NHS works well and people like it as it is (or at least want it tweaked here and re-tuned there, rather than bulldozed); the fact that it gives families who are skint (and there are many) the same health treatment as those who aren't; and of course that, on the whole, patient needs are put first since they don't have to compete with the needs of shareholders.

The pro-privatization lobby would point to the fact that private sector governance automatically brings with it increased efficiency, greater accountability, consumer benefits with improved services, competitive markets and less cost to the taxpayer. And these arguments sound pretty convincing until we look at the recent history of privatization in the UK.

Greater efficiency

In 1990, Conservative MP Geoffrey Howe extolled the 'discipline' of the marketplace, the idea being that privatization would make

266

large utilities more efficient and productive. However, in the arena of transport, privatization has *not* automatically led to greater efficiency. The East Coast franchise is the only franchise run by the public sector; it's also the most efficient in the UK, according to the Office of Rail Regulation.[7] In fact, the publicly owned East Coast line is working better for passengers *and* for taxpayers. In the field of social security, Atos, the private company brought in by the government to assess disability claimants and decide whether they were fit to return to work, have been so efficient that 38% of their decisions about disabled people turned out to be wrong.[8] But that was OK because the boss got a £1 million bonus anyway. I'd have loved to have seen his bonus if he hadn't got any wrong.

Greater accountability

With regard to energy privatization, MPs on the Energy and Climate Change Committee recently reported on energy prices, profits and poverty in a new report.[9] Liberal Democrat Sir Robert Smith MP said: 'At a time when many people are struggling with the rising costs of energy, consumers need reassurance that the profits being made by the Big Six are not excessive. Unfortunately, the complex vertically-integrated structure of these companies means that working out exactly how their profits are made requires forensic accountants.' Apart from that though they are really accountable. When our friends at Atos, mentioned above, were criticized by disability campaigners, they proudly displayed their transparency and accountability credentials by trying to shut down their websites.[10]

It will benefit customers

A recent Europe-wide study found that privatization has had 'largely negative effects on employment and working conditions'. This is because it usually leads to job cuts and the replacement of qualified staff with casual workers, who are paid less and have worse conditions. This of course impacts on the service that people get. In our privatized energy market the fact remains that those who can afford to pay least for their energy still pay the most. A recent survey by 'Which?' that graded customer satisfaction for the UK's top 100 companies showed that the energy companies operating in the UK: nPower,

BT, EDF Energy, British Gas and E.ON — all providing essential utilities, which would have been publicly owned before the 1980s — feature in the top ten worst. That is to say, customers think they are shit. If you are in the company of Poundstretcher and Ryanair for customer satisfaction (also in the bottom ten), you're probably not doing that well. It's like being voted behind Richard Branson in a poll of attractive grins.

The rampant success of our privatized rail network means that fares in France are four times cheaper than in the UK.[11] This is not considered by most UK consumers to be a benefit. Finally, evidence shows that contracting out NHS services — cleaning, GP 'out of hours' services, treatment centres, clinical services and IT has often had a negative effect on the quality of patient care.[12] In the field of health, a recent article in the *British Medical Journal* suggests that the New Labour government's Private Finance Initiative loans to fund hospitals effectively meant the transfer of money from the NHS into private hands. This policy led directly to such customer benefits as a reduction of 73,000 beds (almost a third) between 1992-3 and 2009-10.[13]

It leads to competitive markets

Except that it doesn't really. More often than not it has led to monopolies pretending that they are competitive, getting fined a little bit for being naughty, saying sorry and continuing to act as monopolies to control prices artificially. A recent report by the Institute for Public Policy Research on the cost of energy[14] noted that 'there is a lack of competition in the energy supply market and some consumers are paying over the odds as a result'. This is because, in the energy market, few new players have come to the market post-deregulation, and almost none of those that did make the attempt are still around.

It leads to innovation

The fact is that private companies have 'commercially sensitive' contracts. They tend not to share information with others because to do so loses them a competitive advantage. In the energy sector, deregulation means we still have the same old problems such as billing based on usage estimates despite the fact that in many other countries meters have been read by radio signal for decades and bills are always based on an actual reading. The lack of private investment in our privatized rail network means that the average age of trains is higher than it was in 1996 when it was first privatized.[15]

It costs the taxpayer less

Not true. Value for money goes down because private companies must make a profit for their shareholders and they also pay their top executives more money. This means we, via the government, end up paying more than we did before. Fares on our privatized railways and buses are the most expensive in Europe, while people are also being hit with consistently high energy prices.[16] It has been predicted that the government could save £1.2 billion a year by bringing the railways into public ownership because the direct public spending on rail has more than doubled since privatization.[17]

An assumption that privatization of our health service will automatically make it better is flawed. But that isn't the only matter at hand here. Another key issue is whether the people driving through future changes to a privatized health service will really care about their benefits to patients. I can illustrate this point with a convoluted and probably unnecessary story about a water cooler.

A few years back, I used to work in an office that had a water cooler, until one day two members of staff decided that the machine was environmentally unfriendly and that it had to go. They may well have been right but my problem with this particular green intervention was that these two didn't actually use the machine. Here for them presented a perfect opportunity to display their green credentials and at no price. They didn't stop driving to work and take the train and they didn't stop flying around Europe for their holidays to seriously reduce their carbon footprint. Instead, they decided to get rid of a machine that didn't have any impact on them. Indeed, they said we could just use the tap in the kitchen. This would have been fine except that our particular tap produced water that tasted like it had fallen out of a particularly warm anus. On a good day. (I hasten to point out that these two colleagues weren't using this tap any more frequently than the rest of us. I guess they just weren't big water drinkers.)

Just like my environmentally selective colleagues, the politicians so keen to push through this radical overhaul of the NHS do not understand the role that it has in people's lives. This is because it often doesn't have this role in *their* lives. For some who have the luxury of private health care coverage, the NHS is a gigantic water cooler, dispensing cool, clean water to people who could just as easily use a tap that dispenses rusty, tepid anus water. They do not understand this institution that sits on our shoulder like a big, ugly concrete guardian angel and flutters its underfunded wings when we need it most. They can never understand just what a monumental social invention took place in 1948 when Nye Bevan and colleagues resolved to end the misery of people living with no access to health care.

Here in the UK we haven't always had a great track record when it comes to inventions. The 1975 Hillman Avenger springs to mind here. But where we tend to get it right is in our social innovations, and of all social innovations, those that hold out a hand to people when they are at their most vulnerable, the NHS is the one that we can be most proud of. There's something about our National Health Service that transcends mere health care. It represents one of the last vestiges of virtue and social compassion in a time where our social fabric is being systematically unpicked by those who preach the creed of self-interest.

One aspect of our social lives deserves to be beyond this urge toward self-interest and profit. We haven't managed it with hunger, with poverty or social inequality but we can do it with health. Here we can draw a line that says that, no matter who you are, no matter what circumstances you are in, no matter how much money you do or don't have, you will always receive quality health care free at the point of delivery. This is where we say that we will not let the people of our country live or die in pain because they cannot afford insurance premiums.

The NHS is far from perfect. Sometimes its workers make mistakes and these mistakes can be catastrophic. Sometimes they are rude, inept or careless — in every profession there can always be found such examples. And sometimes we can't get seen by our GPs immediately or get the operation we need straight away. But contrary to the views of the profiteers who perch eagerly on the shoulders of our compromised parliamentarians, and contrary to what some sections of the press would have us believe, the NHS is, on the whole, a really good thing.

References

1. 'The brutal truth about America's healthcare,' *The Independent*, 15 August 2009, available at: www.independent.co.uk/news/world/americas/the-brutal-truth-about-americarsquos-healthcare-1772580.html, accessed 21 March 2014.
2. Figures taken from a 2004 NHS users survey. Cited in Wikipedia on http://en.wikipedia.org/wiki/National–Health–Service–(England)#Public–satisfaction–and–criticism.
3. Colin Pritchard and Mark Wallace, 'Comparing the USA, UK and 17 Western countries' efficiency and effectiveness in reducing mortality,' *Journal of the Royal Society of Medicine*, 2011, 2:60.
4. Randeep Ramesh, 'NHS among developed world's most efficient health systems, says study,' *The Guardian*, 7 August 2011, available at: www.theguardian.com/society/2011/aug/07/nhs-among-most-efficient-health-services, accessed 21 March 2014.
5. 'Income, Poverty, and Health Insurance Coverage in the United States: 2010,' US Census Bureau, issued September 2011. https://www.census.gov/prod/2011pubs/p60-239.pdf
6. Figures taken from CNN.com, 18

September 2009, available at: http://edition.cnn.com/2009/HEALTH/09/18/deaths.health.insurance, accessed 21 March 2014.

7. Taken from 'We Own It' website, http://weownit.org.uk/privatisation accessed 21 March 2014.

8. Ibid.

9. Ibid.

10. The Scottish Association of Citizens Advice Bureaux, 'ATOS should not be able to shut down public debate,' 24 August 2011, http://www.cas.org.uk/news/atos-should-not-be-able-shut-down-public-debate, accessed 21 March 2014

11. Taken from 'We Own It' website, http://weownit.org.uk/privatisation accessed 21 March 2014.

12. Ibid.

13. Ibid.

14. Ibid.

15. Ibid.

16. Ibid.

17. Ibid.

We do hope that you have enjoyed reading this large print book.

Did you know that all of our titles are available for purchase?

We publish a wide range of high quality large print books including:
Romances, Mysteries, Classics
General Fiction
Non Fiction and Westerns

Special interest titles available in large print are:
The Little Oxford Dictionary
Music Book
Song Book
Hymn Book
Service Book

Also available from us courtesy of Oxford University Press:
Young Readers' Dictionary
(large print edition)
Young Readers' Thesaurus
(large print edition)

For further information or a free brochure, please contact us at:
Ulverscroft Large Print Books Ltd.,
The Green, Bradgate Road, Anstey,
Leicester, LE7 7FU, England.
Tel: (00 44) 0116 236 4325
Fax: (00 44) 0116 234 0205

RUNNING LIKE A GIRL

Alexandra Heminsley

Defeated by gyms and bored with yoga, Alexandra Heminsley decided to run — with high hopes of attaining the arse of an athlete, the waist of a supermodel, and the speed of a gazelle. Her first attempt did not end well. Yet, six years later, she had run five marathons in two continents. This is not just a book about running. It's about ambition (getting out of bed on a rainy Sunday morning counts), relationships (including talking to the intimidating staff in the trainer shop), and your body (your boobs *don't* have to wobble when you run). And it's also about realising that you can do more than you ever thought possible . . .

SMOKE GETS IN YOUR EYES

Caitlin Doughty

Most people go to great lengths to avoid thinking about death, but when Caitlin Doughty — a young woman with a degree in medieval history and a flair for the macabre — took a job at Westwind Cremation & Burial, her morbid curiosity turned into her life's work. Leading us behind the black curtain of her profession, Caitlin takes us into a world of vivid characters (both living and deceased) and bizarre details (exactly how a flaming skull looks) — and explores the funeral practices of historic and contemporary cultures, calling for better ways of dealing with death and our dead.

SHOP GIRL

Mary Portas

Young Mary Newton, born into a large Irish family in a small Watford semi, is always getting into trouble. When she isn't choking back fits of giggles at Holy Communion or eating Chappie dog food for a bet, she's accidentally setting fire to the local school. Whilst money is scarce, these are good times, and everything revolves around the force of nature that is Theresa, Mary's mum. But when tragedy unexpectedly blows this world apart, a new chapter in Mary's life opens up. She takes to the camp and glamour of Harrods window dressing like a duck to water — and Mary, Queen of Shops is born . . .